The Deep Places

The Deep Places

*A Memoir of Illness
and Discovery*

Ross Douthat

CONVERGENT
NEW YORK

Published in the United States by Convergent Books,
an imprint of Random House, a division of
Penguin Random House LLC, New York.

CONVERGENT BOOKS is a registered trademark and its C colophon
is a trademark of Penguin Random House LLC.

LIBRARY OF CONGRESS CATALOGING-IN-PUBLICATION DATA
Names: Douthat, Ross Gregory, author.
Title: The deep places / Ross Douthat.
Description: New York : Convergent, [2021]
Identifiers: LCCN 2021024033 (print) | LCCN 2021024034 (ebook) |
ISBN 9780593237366 (hardcover) | ISBN 9780593237373 (ebook)
Subjects: LCSH: Douthat, Ross Gregory—Health. |
Lyme disease—Patients—United States—Biography. | Chronically ill—
United States—Biography. | Journalists—United States—Biography.
Classification: LCC RC155.5 .D68 2021 (print) |
LCC RC155.5 (ebook) | DDC 616.9/2460092 [B]—dc23
LC record available at https://lccn.loc.gov/2021024033
LC ebook record available at https://lccn.loc.gov/2021024034

PRINTED IN CANADA ON ACID-FREE PAPER

crownpublishing.com

2 4 6 8 9 7 5 3 1

First Edition

Illustration by iStock/Nosyrevy

For Abby, again, and always

Maybe somebody has to explore what happens
when one of us wanders over near the edge
and falls for awhile. Maybe it was your turn.

William Stafford, "Afterwards"

FOR A LONG TIME I WOULD ALWAYS WAKE UP EARLY. SOME mornings there would be a moment when I was conscious but not yet fully aware of my body, just a mind floating lightly in the dark. But then very quickly I would feel the weight of things, my legs and chest on the mattress, my head heavy on the pillow. And then quickly too, the pain would be with me once again.

The first sensation was always something different—a heavy ache in the shoulder I'd been sleeping on, a pan-fry sizzle on my hips, a throbbing at the very front of my skull, an intolerable vibration inside my ankles. Then it spread and varied as I pushed back the blanket and fumbled for my phone, shoving my mind into the glowing screen while my body shuttled through its symptoms.

Sometimes I would lie in a cramped position scrolling Twitter, picking up fragments of news, chasing threads of arguments from overnight, letting the pain work through my limbs and joints, watching the clock slowly creep toward 5 A.M. That was on a good morning. On the bad ones, I would be forced up quickly, staggering to the bathroom, leaving Abby to sleep—I hoped—in a snow fort of blankets on the far side of the bed.

The house was old, so very old, but the bathroom was new—an expanse of tile, a shower like a grotto, a his-and-hers sink with drawers for both of us below a sweep of mirror. The floor was even supposed to be heated in the winter, but the system had been on the fritz since we moved in, and the wall panel flickered in the half-light with a gibberish of broken digits.

I moved around the room like an acolyte tending to different altars—now planted on the toilet or hunched over it, now leaning heavily on the glass door of the shower, now standing at the sink staring at my haggard, puffy face. I opened the drawer beneath and fished out a bottle of pills—one bottle among many, filling compartments meant for combs and soap and razors—and swallowed one, two, a handful. After a while they would hit home, and I would shimmy my legs, flail my arms, stretch my face muscles into a silent Munchian scream. Except when the pain was deep, layers down inside my chest, and there was nothing to do but sit with it on the cold, unheated floor.

The light would come up gradually, the clock on my phone creeping on toward six. Eventually I would leave the bathroom, sometimes wrung out and exhausted enough to fade back into a twenty-minute sleep, but sometimes still aching and burning—in which case I would pad through the master bedroom, past my blanketed wife, out onto the landing at the junction of the house's long T-shape.

Through one door our daughters lay asleep, in two identical white beds in a room whose floor sloped downward toward the corner where the foundation had settled, long New England years ago. Through another our infant son stirred in his crib. The hall stretched away down the length of the T, and I followed it, the floor creaking a little, to what had once been a servant's bedroom, sealed away with its own bathroom near a back stairway to the kitchen.

The extra bedroom was supposed to be an office, a place to write away from the noise of kids and the babble of the social life we imagined hosting. I did do a lot of my writing there, on a drop-leaf desk with books stacked around it and a lamp propped up above. But the main thing inside the desk was a further supply of bottles, squat and round for pills and slim for tinctures, stamped with leaves and berries, mosaics and inscriptions, Chinese characters, a dragon chasing his own tail. And beneath the drop-leaf I now stored a box, a black console with buttons in red and green and white and blue, with a tangle of red and black cords running out from it, and metal tubes where the cords ended, just the right size to be gripped in an adult human hand.

On either side of the desk were windows, old colonial frames with slightly mottled glass, looking out and down, offering a view of the landscape in the soft gray morning light. Just below was a wide flagstone patio, with a little lawn pasted in between a white garage and stone steps leading leftward toward a pool. Then the lawn reached a picket fence, beyond which the ground fell away in levels—first a spill of boulders, then an overgrown path, then another drop to a field that went red and brown all winter but came back green with spring. I could see tall grass and cattails rising from a damp low-lying patch, before the pasture climbed to a granite knoll and a single ash tree, a sentinel of the woods that waited just beyond.

The light spread and the landscape brightened, putting on its taunting beauty once again.

I bent to the desk, gripped the metal tubes, and turned on the machine.

CONTENTS

The Deep Places

A Dark Wood

I ALWAYS WANTED TO MOVE BACK TO NEW ENGLAND.
My wife and I both grew up in Connecticut: Abby in
a green town just far enough from New York to count as the
country, me in the rust and brick and Gothic of New Haven.
My mother's family were Maine Yankees from Puritan stock
with a solid three-century history of staying put in chilly soil.
My wife's ancestors were from Newfoundland and Ireland,
cold seacoasts and autumnal skies. As kids, we both made the
long drive to Maine in the summers—in my case to the coastline where my grandparents lived and my uncle and cousins
worked as lobstermen, in her case to a Girl Scout camp way
up in the North Woods, cabins speckling the shores of a deep-
blue lake under the shadow of Katahdin, the highest mountain in the state.

So living in the humid marshland of Washington, D.C.,
where we ended up together and married in our twenties,
always felt like a mistake. The Mid-Atlantic was almost like
the Northeast, but just slightly different in its temperature
and color schemes—more sweltering in the summer and less
vivid in the fall, with more winter rain and June warmth
than our remembered childhood worlds. I would have pre-

ferred a stark contrast, the prairie or the Rockies or the Californian chaparral. Instead the resemblance just reinforced our mutual homesickness for deep woods and colonial houses, birches and evergreens, old stone walls and blizzards.

Then we had children, two daughters two years apart, and the drives back to see our families became harder, the nostalgia more intense. We lived in Capitol Hill, ten blocks from the Capitol dome, in a small row house in a gentrifying neighborhood. But once we had the kids the house felt tiny, the frequent terror alerts exhausting, the Beltway traffic between Ikea and Buy Buy Baby grueling. When we looked to the future, to more children and more space, the local school environment seemed punishingly competitive, an enemy of childhood. And the prices in the D.C. suburbs, for houses that we didn't even like, were utterly insane.

I had a romantic idea of the alternative. My own parents had grown up in beautiful places, my mother in a farmhouse on a saltwater cove and my dad near the beach in Santa Monica, but when I was young they ended up living in a blue-collar corner of New Haven, in a ranch-house neighborhood that didn't measure up to their memories of natural beauty. My mother pined for rocky coasts and spruce trees and high blue skies. My father missed the smell of eucalyptus. So I inherited an idea about land, beautiful land, as something intimately connected to the good life, yet always tantalizingly out of reach.

But by the time I turned thirty-five, it wasn't out of reach anymore. Our row house, bought after the financial crisis, had appreciated absurdly in four years. I had a job as a *New York Times* columnist—a lucky opportunity, a dream job— that basically allowed me to live anywhere, so long as there was an internet connection and a way to fly or ride to Washington and New York. Many of the young families we knew talked about fleeing D.C. for their hometowns, or settling in some small, livable city, or even buying a Virginia farm. But for us the temptation was particularly sharp. We wanted to have another baby; my wife had just left her magazine job to write her first book. Why shouldn't we blaze the trail, make the fantasy real?

So we began taking the possibility seriously. We followed Connecticut real estate listings with an increasing obsessiveness, and whenever we headed north to visit our families, we made time for long drives through the country, letting our girls nap while we scoped out likely-seeming towns and random open houses. Eventually we took a more consistent approach with an actual realtor—although we were still haphazard enough in our visits that the agent, a polished Englishwoman whose daughters rode horses, regarded our intentions with a certain suspicion, as though she'd seen dreamers like us before.

Abby tried to keep us grounded. We wanted the same general things, but she was a little less romantic about rural life. "It's way too uncanny to imagine actually living there," she said to me after a day trip through small towns in the northern part of the state, outposts of New York City for their summer residents, farm towns in the winter. "There's nobody there half the year, who knows what the schools are like, we'd be two hours from New York, forty minutes from our parents . . . and you're going to leave me alone in the country with the kids while you go traveling for work?"

Honestly that was, in a way, my treasured plan. I had a vision of myself going out into the world, flying around to various Babylons for important meetings and interviews, and then coming home on a summer evening, down a winding road, up a drive lined with oak trees, to find my two—no, make it three; no, make it *four*—kids waiting for me, playing on swings in the July dusk in front of a big white colonial, my wife behind them, the whole scene an Arcadia . . .

Not surprisingly, Abby wasn't sold on this idyll, or the alleged bargains I kept finding—the snowbound spread on six acres with a leaking roof and a huge artist's studio attached; the "farmhouse" built into a hillside like a hobbit's hole, if a hobbit had an investment banker's taste. The first Connecticut house that she actually liked was far more sensible: a recent build in a more populated area, a four-bedroom house from the 1950s, at the end of a quiet cul-de-sac near a commuter rail station, walkable to a playground and a small downtown. It was lovely, livable, convenient, a good size for a growing family. I hated it.

"It looks like Tony Soprano's house!" I groused. "You can see McMansions from the kitchen window! What's the point of going to Connecticut for something we can get in"—I let the contempt flow through me—"*suburban Virginia?*"

Eventually, like a good husband, I started to talk myself into the sensible house. But by then, like a generous wife, she had talked herself out of it.

Fortunately, there was an area where our ideas converged, which happened to be her childhood hometown. It was just ninety minutes from Manhattan, in between the Gold Coast of greater Greenwich and the small blue-collar cities and real country to the north. It was near enough to train lines to be accessible to the city, far enough to be relatively affordable. It had a rural expanse but a thriving downtown with a bookstore and restaurants and even a small movie theater. It had excellent public schools and a lovely little Catholic church, where we had been married.

Moving there with our children, buying a big house, and making ourselves comfortable with Little League games and dance lessons felt like a way to rewrite the story of Abby's childhood as well. She had lived in a big house once: Her father had been a Wall Street numbers guy who descended into bankruptcy and ruin after the junk-bond era collapsed. He died suddenly when she was thirteen, leaving her schoolteacher mother to raise Abby and her sister alone. So her hometown had been for her a place of downward mobility, of childhood happiness succeeded by teenage sorrow. And it seemed (maybe more to me than to her) that to return in prosperity and triumph would give her the happy ending she deserved.

"Unless you lose your job," she said. "Or we lose all our money."

"That could happen in D.C., too," I countered. "And in Connecticut we'll have our family to help us, public schools . . . We'll raise chickens *and* join Costco."

So her doubts gradually yielded to my optimism, and then in the winter of 2015 we endured a sequence of what seemed at the time like hardships—the teacher at our older daughter's local public pre-K quit suddenly, our basement flooded when frozen pipes exploded, my wife and a friend were mugged while they strolled a baby in the nearby park— that felt almost like providential pushes to *sell, just sell,* to take the money and flee north.

For Abby, the decisive tribulation happened just outside our home. We had to parallel-park our SUV on the street outside our front door, and every once in a while a car would come barreling down the mostly quiet street when we were hauling our girls, four and two, out of their car seats to the safety of the sidewalk. One slushy March day, when the piles of unmelted snow further shrank the narrow street, one of these cars veered within inches of my wife as she fumbled with a car seat, almost dinging the open door behind her, and then slammed to a halt ten yards on, disgorging a furious driver who yelled *at Abby* for being so inconveniently available to be mowed down.

"Right then and there, I thought, *I don't want to die on this stupid street,*" she said to me afterward, as we huddled over my laptop and the real estate listings in her once and future hometown.

So we went ahead and did it. We put our house on the market in the spring, working with a raffish, chain-smoking broker who wrote his listings in rhyming couplets and had a genius for instigating bidding wars. And we began shuttling back and forth to Connecticut every weekend to look at houses, in the town and just outside it, new and old, still looking for the one that fit our idea of what a New England house should be: something suitably antique and white-shingled, ideally with a barn and a field, but also ideally with a decent kitchen—you know, *updated*—and rooms that didn't feel like they were built for the seventeenth century's average height.

Meanwhile in D.C., the raffish broker worked his magic and our row house sold for more than even we had dared to hope. I had some sort of pompous D.C. dinner the night the deal went through, and I remember *skipping* down the side-walk on my way back home, wine flowing in my blood-stream, giddy as a gambler who's just raked in a table's worth of winnings.

Leaning in to the excitement, which our Connecticut realtor naturally shared, we expanded our price range to in-clude a bunch of over-a-million-dollar houses that we had previously ruled out. One of them was a 1790s farmhouse, its long colonial shape adorned at one end with Greek revival pillars, with three acres of pastureland, a barn and an apple tree, a guest cottage and a pool. It felt like it was in the country, but it was a five-minute drive to Main Street—even walkable, we assured ourselves, though we hadn't tried to make the walk. The property needed work, lots of work, but the main house was in good shape. "You could even get an *agricultural tax exemption*," our realtor said encouragingly as we peered into the vacant chicken coop out back.

It was expensive—a definite reach—but in the years it had been on (and off, and on) the market the price had plummeted, and we had help with the repairs. My wife's mother lived ten minutes away; my father and his soon-to-be second wife, twenty minutes. They were encouraging; they had time on their hands and they would help us. Interest rates were low, and the cottage had a tenant, which supplied a rental-income stream.

Besides, we were young and energetic and healthy, and a reach was what I particularly wanted—a place that would force me outside, tear me away from the vortex of the internet, the tyranny of the screen, the sedentary pundit's life. I planned to mow lawns, tear up bushes, rebuild tumbled stone walls. Maybe I would even plant a garden with my daughters.

And truth be told, I didn't really think of it as a reach at all, because at that moment in my life I only really believed in upside. My childhood inheritance included reasonably strong Christian beliefs, and my profession required me to comment frequently on religion, which meant that during our years in Washington I wrote my share of words on the problem of evil—the why-does-God-let-bad-things-happen-to-good-people question—usually making the case that much of American Christianity offers people the wrong answers, encouraging them to believe that actually bad things shouldn't happen if you're good, that the American Dream should be yours if you just stay in God's good graces and follow the paths that He's marked out, as straight as I-95 running north.

I had a similar critique of the secular meritocracy in which I had been educated: that because it asked its climbers to work so hard and jump so high, it encouraged an idea that we had somehow earned all our privileges, that our SAT scores and extracurricular accomplishments meant that we genuinely deserved to rule.

But despite these critiques, there was still a sense in which I believed exactly these ideas myself—or at least *for* myself— as I passed through college into adulthood, achieved the career as a writer that I wanted, won the wife I wanted, the job I wanted, the kids I wanted, and now the house and country life I wanted, too.

"It's really impressive, Ross," an ex-military friend of mine said when we chatted about our big move. "You guys set this goal and you did it. You just did it."

That was basically how I thought of myself at that point in my life. I was the guy who *did* things. My ancestral line was filled with failed businessmen and artistic types, garage-sale rummagers and self-conscious outsiders—the sort of educated people who used the *Times* stock market listings for kindling on family picnics to show their disdain for upper-class success. I always intended to be different, and I always had been, from the Harvard acceptance letter to the job at the *Times,* and now to this brilliant real estate coup that would root us securely in a family compound for decades to come. So the way it happened, the sale and the opportunity coming together, felt like confirmation that we were on the right path, that I had planned and worked and won the things I wanted and that I deserved them—that my ambitions and God's purposes could stroll along together nicely, that bad things might sometimes happen to good meritocrats, but surely not to me.

It rained on the day of the house inspection, and the list of fixes the inspectors produced was daunting—chimney repairs, rot in the barn, gutters that needed replacing, a damp spot in the basement, on and on. I walked down the overgrown path below the house, the dripping branches stroking my shoulders as I watched a family of deer dart through the meadow. Then I looked up at the main building, perched above the pastures like a ship riding stormy seas.

Yes, I thought, *this is what I want.*

MY MOTHER DROVE THE HOUR FROM NEW HAVEN TO SEE the house that weekend. She was a little less enthusiastic than my father and Abby's mom—I assumed because we were planting ourselves a little farther away from her. She also had health problems that made her sensitive to things like mold and damp and the age of the buildings. I sensed that she wanted to warn us away from the house, but since she knew we were committed, she was instead exhibiting vague signs of distress. After we parted, she drove by the house once again, then called that night to tell me that she'd seen a stag relieving himself near our soon-to-be front door.

Soon after, at her house, my childhood home, she encountered another deer, standing on her property near where she was pulling out some bushes—much as I aspired to do.

Her neighborhood is not particularly bucolic; we had raccoons and squirrels when I was a kid, but in twenty years she had never seen a deer.

Later that week, when she was working in the same area, just where the deer had been standing, she almost stepped through a thin sheet of rusted metal, flush to the ground beneath a thin layer of soil. When she lifted it, there was an opening into a frighteningly deep void or cave, maybe left over from some ancient fuel tank or septic system—an empty space inside the hillside, a dark and earthy pit.

BY THIS TIME ABBY AND I WERE BACK IN WASHINGTON, with a two-month timeline to closing and taking possession of our dream house. This would free up the entire summer for shuttling north on weekends and playing at renovation, pulling up carpets and refinishing floors and tearing out the bushes that blocked the sunroom's views.

It was another rainy morning. I awoke with a stiff neck and went to the bathroom to find a red swelling, a painful lymph node six inches down from my left ear. I came out and sat on the bed, rubbing my neck and googling "swollen lymph node" on my phone.

My wife came in, behind me, her voice unusual: "Ross."

She was holding a pregnancy test, the telltale strip faint but clear. Our third child.

It should have been another signifier that we were on the right path, on the upswing—more kids, more life, more abundance. But after I fist-pumped and we embraced, after I said all the right excited things, after I went out into the rain to take our daughters to their nursery school and pre-K, my mind and fingers kept circling back to the discomfort in my neck.

I had seen a dermatologist for a wart the previous year, but he didn't have an appointment available for a week, and I was impatient. I wanted the problem—however small—explained and resolved so that we could get back to basking in our triumphs. So instead of waiting to see him, I went that day to the urban walk-in clinic in the heart of Capitol Hill, walking through our dense neighborhood with its pocket parks and carefully controlled daubs of natural green, and let a young internist take a look.

"It's just a boil," he said after a cursory inspection. "Nothing to worry about." He gave me a scrip for a few days of a mild antibiotic, and sent me on my way.

Nothing to worry about was exactly what I wanted to hear. The next two weeks were less soothing. While we did paperwork and drove to Connecticut and back again, my neck began to feel intermittently stiff and painful and I developed what felt like a . . . *vibration* in my head. Still, the original swelling shrank and disappeared, and I told myself that the strange feelings, the tension and the almost-tremor, were probably stress-induced, just all the life changes piling atop one another and giving me the jitters. Something like that had happened six years earlier: When we were first married and I was commuting back and forth from Washington to Baltimore, there had been a period of odd headaches, pain in my neck and back, that after a few inconclusive doctor's visits had simply vanished, unexplained but attributed, shruggingly, to the stress of my new life and the commute.

Now it was early June, and I was supposed to join a journalists' trip to Rome. On the day before the flight, I went to see a movie and, sitting in the theater, I noticed that the pain was getting worse: There was a stabbing sensation in my mouth, around my teeth, and discomfort sharp enough to call a headache. My mother-in-law arrived that evening, planning to help with the kids while I was gone. She and my wife went out to dinner; I stayed home to put my daughters to bed. I made some pasta for myself and drank two beers. It was my last ordinary meal.

By the time Abby and her mother got home, my whole body was just . . . *wrong,* haywire somehow, as though someone had twisted dials randomly in all my systems. I told them I wasn't feeling well, as if I had a stomach flu or something that might pass by the morning, and let them fall asleep believing in that understatement. But I didn't sleep: I had pain all over my chest and a gagging feeling in my throat, and the vibratory sensation was everywhere. My bowels had liquefied. I googled "heart attack" and "stroke" and "panic attack," but nothing seemed to fit. I lay down and tried to sleep, but I felt like a tuning fork on the mattress. I went downstairs and tried to read books and take deep breaths. Finally at 5 A.M. I went to the hospital—the George Washington University emergency room, in downtown D.C.

While I was there the wave receded, and I felt weak and exhausted but at least somewhat like myself. The blood tests came back normal, the doctors murmured about stress—one of them recognized my name from the op-ed page—and around noontime I went home again, trying to decide whether I could travel. In the end I decided to cancel the trip; I remember thinking, somewhat idiotically, that at least I would get to watch the latest episode of *Game of Thrones.* I went to Mass and prayed for help. I googled neurologists. I managed to sleep.

The next day I felt the way you feel in the last days of a lingering fever, or when you get up too suddenly and feel slightly dizzy and disoriented. Except this feeling persisted no matter what I did. The pain that had started in my neck was jumping around, ubiquitous but unpredictable—now stabbing sensations in my spine, now muscle twitches on my chest, now prickling and tingling in my extremities. And beneath it was a feeling that was hard to describe except as a sense of *invasion,* of something under my skin and inside my veins and muscles that wasn't supposed to be there. This baseline feeling wasn't incapacitating, but it made me feel miserable all the time. For the week after my initial collapse I did ordinary things—driving, walking, grocery shopping, stroller pushing—under a weight of pain, an extraordinary pall.

So I began going to doctors and taking tests. I saw an internist, a neurologist, a rheumatologist. I had my stool and urine tested repeatedly, I had batteries of blood work done, I underwent cranial and abdominal scans and a tilt table test. The only irregular result came from the neurologist, who told me I had some sort of peripheral neuropathy, some kind of interference between the brain and the nerves in my extremities. It would resolve, he suggested, with more exercise and more hydration. (*Maybe drink more Gatorade—for the electrolytes.*) Inspired, I bought new running shorts and shoes—but I felt too horrible to use them. The other doctors prescribed sleeping pills and mild antidepressants and Xanax. *Stress,* they said. It was always stress. *Too much going on in your life.*

I did feel stressed now, but the illness felt like the reason rather than the symptom. I had never been sick for more than a week or so, but there was a shadow from my childhood that with every day of pain and mystery loomed larger in my thoughts. My mother had struggled with chronic illness when I was young, with chemical sensitivities and debilitating inflammation that had sent our family down a lot of strange paths—to health food stores in the days before Whole Foods, to Pentecostalist healing services where people spoke in tongues, to chiropractors and naturopaths and other purveyors of holistic medicine. So I knew something about the country of illness, at least as observed from its borderlands—how a person can be exiled there, how much can be lost or given up. *I will restore to you the years that the swarming locust has eaten:* That was one of my mother's favorite scripture verses, as she tried to make sense of her younger life and its many might-have-beens.

Growing up inside her story left me open to religious possibilities, heterodox ideas, a world that was stranger than official thinking allowed. But as a personal matter I had prided myself on being pretty much nothing like her. I was entirely healthy, entirely *normal,* with no tofu or carob in my diet, no need for herbal remedies or a laying on of hands. I had been an adult in the world for seventeen years, and with a few exceptions my body had done everything I asked of it without complaint—even if my belly had grown a little ample in the process. Having that same body betray me somehow—no, that was unimaginable.

If I had crossed the border into illness, it had to be temporary. It was a mistake, an accident, a passport problem—and I simply had to find the quickest way back out.

AROUND THIS TIME, *NEW YORK* MAGAZINE PUBLISHED A first-person account by a physician who had lived with undiagnosed Lyme disease for years, eventually acquiring a heart condition that required a transplant. The story came with an illustration of a man's body spiderwebbed with brown filaments, like something out of H. P. Lovecraft.

The picture illustrated what I was feeling. The mysterious symptomology seemed similar to mine; the boil on my neck could have been a tick bite. My Lyme test had been reported as a negative, like all the other blood tests, but I obtained a copy and saw that one of the five "bands" that activate in the presence of Lyme antibodies had activated in my test. You need all five for a positive diagnosis, under CDC criteria, but nonetheless I became temporarily obsessed with the idea, in the way of mysteriously ill people with internet connections, setting out to piece together a diagnosis on their own.

Abby was open to strange possibilities: The book she was working on was a natural history of the house cat, and while I was reading the doctor's Lyme testimony she was busy editing a chapter about the mysteries of toxoplasmosis, a parasite carried in cat poop that was known to infiltrate the human brain with all kinds of poorly understood effects. But at this point she was more worried about worst-case scenarios, conditions that could bring our whole life crashing down, the ones that all my varied tests were trying to rule out: cancer, brain tumor, the onset of some obscure degenerative disease. We were children of Connecticut, we knew something about Lyme, but mostly we knew that it involved a rash and achy knees and that it was usually treatable, which kept it pretty far down her list of worries.

And then, too, I wasn't exactly the outdoorsy type, especially compared to my science-writer wife, who had recently stalked endangered red foxes through the marshes of South Carolina and tracked lynx in the Montana snows. I had been outside for, what, ten minutes at the house inspection? What were the odds?

They were low, I conceded. But at that moment it was my strongest theory, and so I took the Lyme hypothesis to the internist I had been assigned as a primary care physician after my ER visit, a kind but harried-seeming young doctor working in the George Washington University hospital system.

"I did have somebody with Lyme last year," she said. "They got it hiking in the Shenandoah. But we don't really get any cases in D.C., and you said you haven't really been outdoors much, right?"

"I mean, yeah, I would have had to get it just from taking one walk around the property we're buying, so it's a little bit of a long shot."

I was trying for a tone that acknowledged how unlikely it sounded, thus projecting reasonability, thus encouraging her to actually prescribe the drugs for me. In only a few weeks of doctor visits, I had already figured out that when you're claiming symptoms that don't show up on blood tests, it's a good idea to exaggerate your own good sense and self-awareness, to keep a smooth veneer over the bubbling *help me, please* hysteria beneath.

"Well, sometimes it can take a while for the blood tests to pick it up—and if you take an antibiotic and get rid of it quickly, I think maybe it never shows up at all. So maybe wait and we'll do another test in a couple weeks?"

"Well, I could, but I don't *really* want to wait," I said, still extremely casual. "Is there any harm in just trying the basic antibiotic course? It's three weeks, right . . . ?"

"Actually, I'm pretty sure the new guidelines say that ten days should be fine to clear anything up," she told me absently. But then, generously: "I'll give you two weeks of doxycycline. The main side effect is sunburn. Let's see how it goes."

I took it. For one day, exactly one day, I felt strangely better, and felt a surge of hope that this was a dark dream that would quickly pass. Then I started getting more stomach pain, with gagging and vomiting, which I assumed was a side effect of the drug. Then the other symptoms returned and my baseline seemed unchanged. So after a week I stopped the doxycycline, suddenly gripped by paranoia (again, in the way of chronically ill people with internet connections) about what the antibiotic might be doing to me.

Instead I veered in a different direction. I decided to try being holistic, experimental, going back to things I remembered from my childhood, my family's vegetarian years and forays into alternative medicine. I abandoned not just junk food but gluten and sugar and dairy, and I made an appointment with a naturopath. It was the first of many desperate, flailing things that I kept temporarily secret from Abby, who was now being carried under by morning sickness as well as anxiety over my condition. To her (or so I imagined) I was mostly reassuring: *I'm functional, I'm functional, I'll be all right.*

And I *was* functional, in the sense that, despite the doctors implying that this was somehow in my head, my mind seemed like the only part of me that worked. I could still write columns, well enough and normally enough that I didn't have to tell my editors how awful I was feeling. I could go on television and talk about American politics; that was the summer when Donald Trump descended the Trump Tower escalator and the election became a fever dream as well. And I could think about my illness, could analyze my symptoms with what seemed like my old familiar reasoning powers, even if my self-diagnosis kept shifting based on which thread or message board I read.

The naturopath worked out of the basement of a downtown apartment building not far from the Watergate. He had a close-cropped beard and the taut skin of the unnaturally healthy. I expected him to dismiss antibiotics, to talk about mind-body connections and recommend meditation. Instead he listened to my story and said he thought the Lyme possibility was a likely one, and that I should go back on doxycycline and finish the course. He also gave me a brace of antimicrobial herbs that were supposed to make antibiotics more effective, and ordered another round of blood tests.

So I went back on doxycycline. This time, with the herbs, something different happened: Incredibly strong waves of pain, stronger than anything before, concentrated especially in my joints, my knees and elbows. The pain seemed to impel me to stomp around, like a restless horse, to walk the streets for miles, as though I were trying to force something out of myself, to burn it and shake it from my tissue.

Reading online, I encountered descriptions of what's called the Jarisch-Herxheimer effect, the sudden flares of symptoms that can accompany the large-scale death of bacteria inside the bloodstream. Named for two nineteenth-century German doctors who identified it in syphilis patients treated with penicillin, it was supposed to be common in Lyme patients as well, at least according to internet testimonials. So I tried to be encouraged by the feeling, treating it as confirmation of my working diagnosis.

That weekend we drove from D.C. to Pittsburgh, my pregnant wife and my suffering body and our two daughters, to visit Abby's sister and her new boyfriend. Halfway there, somewhere in the Appalachians, I began getting crushing pain across my chest, running up through my left shoulder and into my arm. We stopped at a rest stop, and in the bathroom I once again googled "heart attack." The results were predictably unhelpful, so I came out and pretended to be fine: "I just need to walk around for a minute," I said, and I circled the parking lot on foot, letting the wind buffet me, looking west to where the highway descended from the mountains, willing the pain to go away.

It diminished a little, I took the wheel, we drove for thirty minutes, and then it was back, a blaze across my pectoral muscles, and there was nothing to do but tell Abby—quietly, quietly, so the kids couldn't hear us—that I was having really bad chest pain, bad enough that she had to take the wheel. Which she did, after another rest stop interlude, maintaining a maternal calm that was somehow more terrifying than panic, and when we reached Pittsburgh she dropped me at an emergency room while she rushed to settle the girls at our hotel and meet her little sister's future spouse alone, amid Thai carryout and confusion.

There was nothing wrong with my heart, the doctors said, no problems anywhere that they could see. They pushed strange liquids through my system, rolled me under sensors, talked sympathetically to me and skeptically to one another. I lay wrecked in the ER bed. Surely this was the low point, I thought; surely now recovery would begin.

I was wrong. I made it to our hotel room late that night, slept for an hour, strove for normalcy. But then it all fell apart: I sweated through a visit to the Pittsburgh Zoo with the kids, clutching at my left shoulder as the pain built again, and built, and built, and finally I was back at the ER in the evening for the same tests, the same diagnosis, the same sympathetic but disbelieving attitudes.

Somehow we made it back to D.C., to find the results of the naturopath's blood test waiting: negative for Lyme. He thought some secondary tests he had ordered were suspicious, and recommended that I send my blood to a specialty lab. But I had already called my internist, and she had dismissed out of hand the idea that the combination of Lyme and doxycycline could possibly cause phantom heart attacks. ("The Herxheimer . . . ?" I said diffidently. "That shouldn't last more than a day," she said authoritatively.)

So I switched theories: If the latest pain wasn't a heart attack, its location meant it must be heartburn, an ulcer, or some other stomach problem radiating through my chest, and I needed to start chewing Tums and go see a gastroenterologist.

To get doctors quickly, I was using Zocdoc, a website that lets you find any available appointment anywhere in a given radius, and the first gastroenterologist with an opening was way out in the suburbs of Maryland, in a mostly immigrant community. He greeted me with some puzzlement: *How were you referred to me again?* Still, he listened to my story, seemed to accept my basic reasonability—another successful performance of normality, I thought—and ordered up an endoscopy, an inspection of my stomach that was carried out under full anesthesia, a first-ever experience for me, in a clinic that seemed to work like an assembly line, with a jam-packed waiting room where Abby and I were the only people not speaking Tagalog or Spanish.

The anesthesia itself was an unexpected pleasure. I came up from it into a period of hazy relaxation, where I was half-awake but none of my symptoms were palpable, and the still-drugged portion of my mind found itself walking on a bright beach, to the crash of waves.

The test itself, though, found the expected: nothing.

While I was in the recovery room, the doctor took my wife aside. "Has your husband ever considered cognitive behavioral therapy? Because, look—I don't know what's wrong with him, but from what he told me, at this point he should be looking for some kind of psychological help."

IT TOOK A FEW DAYS BEFORE SHE SHARED THIS CONVERSAtion. By now the chest pain was with me constantly, for hours every night and day. Sometimes it came over me when I was watching our little girls, making me terrified that they might have to watch their father collapse in front of them. The fear of dying was subsumed by a fear of failing them, leaving them alone. Sometimes the pain forced me to sit up for hours in the night, clutching my chest and trying to decide whether this time I needed to rush off to the ER again.

Apart from the round of doctors, by now my world had shrunk to just three adults—my wife and, by phone, my divorced parents. I was sure that my mother and father both believed that I was sick in my body, not just mentally unwell. They had enough experience with chronic health problems to be sympathetic rather than skeptical, and they kept trying to connect me to doctors in the Northeast—my mother to a Yale specialist who had helped her long ago, my dad to a friend of his who studied Lyme disease for a New York hospital. But that kind of far-flung connection was beyond me at this point.

And Abby—well, her primal experience of male illness had been her father's depression and psychological descent, which meant that when doctors told me (or murmured to her) that it might all be a mental perturbation, the diagnosis felt familiar and horribly plausible. I could tell that she wanted to believe me, to believe in the reality of my physical symptoms, to take my side against all the doubting experts. But she also had a journalist's natural skepticism, and even though she was writing about natural history at the moment, her fundamental interest as a reporter had always been the mysteries of the human personality. So inevitably she found herself probing, pushing at the hypotheses and theories that I was cycling through, asking if this or that thing that I tried was making me feel better. Behind her questions I could hear the voices of her friends, good and reasonable and sensible people all, to whom she was obliged to explain *what was wrong with Ross* in a way that didn't make me just sound crazy, and from whom, I could tell, she was getting advice that maybe didn't use words like *nervous breakdown* but certainly tiptoed close.

I wanted to reassure her, but in practice that meant just playing my part in a grim call-and-response when I was up at night groaning in the bathroom . . .

Ross, are you all right?

I'm all right, please get some sleep, I'll be all right . . .

I obviously wasn't, but by this point I was deep into self-doubt about the reality of my experience. On the one hand, there was the pain, the burning, the vibrations, the feeling of invasion; I knew I'd never felt anything like this before. But what were mere feelings set against the certainties of so many doctors, the repeated negative readings of my blood? I could list reasons why a rational person, standing outside my situation, would conclude that I was a good candidate for a psychosomatic illness, a stress-induced breakdown. I had a high-pressure job, a writer's temperament, a flair for the dramatic, a family history of unusual sensitivities. I had that week of mysterious pain six years earlier as an antecedent. I was religious; God knows religious people were always inclined to have "experiences" that were mostly in their heads.

Of course, there were also counterarguments. I was religious in an intellectual sense, but not remotely mystical (I had been an observer of strange experiences in my childhood, but never a participant), and I was one of the most emotionally well-balanced people in my social circle, with no history of depression and a fundamental personal optimism that always surprised people who knew me only from my pessimistic columns. ("The difference between us, Ross," a friend told me once, in frustration at my evident enjoyment of a particularly gloomy autumn day, "is that you *like* melancholy, but I *am* melancholy.") I had never experienced a lengthy illness, and my decline was steep rather than gradual. As for stress, what sort of stress-induced illness would manifest itself at a moment of apparent triumph, a successful real estate transaction and literal dream-come-true escape?

Finally, there was the pain, whose reality was brutally palpable even if I couldn't demonstrate its existence with blood work or brain scans. Like Samuel Johnson kicking a rock to disprove the philosophy of immaterialism, I should have been able to lie back, experience the burning, the chest pain, the tingling in the extremities, and tell all the *it's all in your head* doctors, "I refute you *thus.*"

But I didn't have that confidence. Night after night, day after day, my self-belief was worn away, pushing me toward submission to the medical system's diagnoses, encouraging me to act as if the psychosomatic interpretation was the truth.

The tipping point was my session with the most prominent doctor that I contrived to see, the head of infectious diseases at a major Washington, D.C., hospital, an appointment that took six weeks to get and that lasted all of fifteen minutes. He looked at my charts, listened to an abbreviated version of my story, sighed, and leaned backward in his chair.

"Look, Debra did everything for you here," he said. (Debra was the internist who had run my tests and given me the doxycycline.) "There just aren't any other tests to do. If you had an infection, we'd catch it."

By now my facade of reasonability was thinner. I just bent my head and said weakly, "So what does that mean? I'm just in so much pain, Doctor. Can it really all be just stress?"

He shrugged and spread his hands, like a simple country vicar asked to explain the Holy Trinity. "There's just a lot we don't understand about the human body. A lot of *mystery,* you know? But look, you're young and healthy. I'm sure you'll feel better."

"I wish I felt sure."

"Well, I'm older than you, I've seen people in a lot worse shape. The important thing here is that we can rule certain things out—that's what we do here. And look, I know it's hard to see, but you should feel happy. It's a good thing not to have a disease, you know."

Then, into the awkward silence: "And if you need a mental-health referral, we can *definitely* help with that."

SO I WENT AT LAST TO A PSYCHIATRIST, MY ELEVENTH DOC-tor in ten weeks. He let me pour out my story for an hour, and then he told me that in his experience the kind of physical symptoms I was experiencing had to have some real physiological root, some cause beyond stress or psychosomatic collapse.

But now I was committing to the anxiety diagnosis. I did a phone appointment with a kind of "healer" who had helped one of my relatives with anxiety in her movie-business career; he told me that what was happening to me was all about my age, the transition from youth into my late thirties, and probably some long-buried issues with my father. I scoured books about anxiety, looking for accounts of people who exhibited physical as well as mental symptoms, for stories about nervous disorders that affected the nerves in a literal, painful, fiery way. I emailed an old colleague who had written a book on his own anxiety disorder, asking for a referral to the clinic that had helped him. I acquired a set of exercises called "the healing power of breath," and at night, while my wife slept or tried to sleep beside me, I did its exercises with quiet desperation, trying to relax myself into more than a few minutes of real sleep. And when the waves of pain came over me, as strong as ever, I told myself that none of it was real, that I was just being stabbed by a dagger of the mind.

My memories of that August are scant. I remember going in to CNN for a TV hit and running into Donna Brazile, the Democratic strategist, who remarked on how much weight I'd lost.

"I'm having a nervous breakdown," I told her, all filters on my honesty removed. "We're leaving D.C."

She looked startled, and then gave me a generous smile. "Best thing to do," she said. "This city drives everyone insane."

At home, I wasn't sleeping at all, an hour a night at most, despite a raft of prescriptions from various doctors for anxiety and sleep. I would drift off and suddenly be pulled awake, usually by a feeling like an alarm clock going off in my chest, almost *lifting* me into consciousness, and sometimes, and more horribly, by the feeling that my throat was closing up.

Somehow we packed up our house in Capitol Hill. I said goodbye to almost none of our friends; I was too sick and Abby too exhausted, too baffled by what had happened to her usually healthy, usually optimistic spouse. With my stomach, throat, and bowels all afire, I had stopped eating as well as sleeping, and lost forty pounds in just ten weeks. In one of the few pictures taken in our last days in D.C., I look skeletal and permeable, like a haunted-house ghost accidentally captured by a tourist's camera.

Somehow we made the long drive to Connecticut and began the process of moving into our new house, which sprawled, lovely and rambling—exactly the late-summer vision that I had imagined, but now seen through a veil of pain.

My hands shook when I acquired the check for the closing and signed the final papers. I told myself that maybe all the anxiety would pass once we were inside, the move accomplished, the chasm leaped.

I was wrong. On the day we took possession, I wandered down the hill and out into the field, to stand and look back up toward the house. The girls were inside playing, running through the empty rooms, building forts with cardboard boxes. My father and mother-in-law were in and out, looking over all the things that had been accomplished in the past two months, old bedroom carpets torn out and the downstairs bathroom retiled and the curtain of shrubbery around the sunroom ripped away—some of which my dad had done himself, some of which I had arranged in phone calls with contractors at prices that I could only hazily recall. There was a simple familial joy at work for everyone else, a feeling of taking possession, coming into an unexpected inheritance, and even my worried, exhausted wife was caught up in it. I still have the video of Abby walking through the house that day, beaming and gesturing grandly at the home that she now owned.

It was exactly what I had envisioned when we first started combing rural listings—and really long before that, as far back as childhood, when I had imagined myself as an owner of a big old house, the sort of rambling place where the kids in children's stories are forever making discoveries, magical wardrobes and secret gardens and treasure maps inside the walls.

But I felt none of it. What I did feel that first day, apart from the pain across my shoulders and down my arms that made it hard for me to open windows or assemble cribs, was a new fear to go along with all the anxieties of the last three awful months—a fear of financial ruin, which hung over the broken fences, the sagging barn, the unfenced pool, everything we'd paid for so far and everything that still needed to be done.

By the time I realized that I was really sick, we had closed on our D.C. home and were a huge chunk of earnest money deep into the Connecticut house. There had never seemed to be any option except to go ahead, to hope that family help and my eventual recovery would carry us into our new life.

But we were here, I wasn't better, and when I looked at our new home now, it seemed to rear up like a house in a very different kind of childhood story—its antique bulk a repository for darkness, its open doors and windows an invitation to come inside and never leave again.

.   .   .

I HAD AN APPOINTMENT THAT FIRST WEEK WITH A CON-
necticut psychiatrist, who I hoped would at least re-up my
battery of anxiety medications and sleeping pills. She listened, took notes, and said, "I'm pretty sure you have a tick-
borne illness, Ross. It sounds like the doctors down where
you've been living don't see a lot of cases. But up here, this
all sounds familiar."

The next day I saw the local family doctor whose practice
had been recommended to us. "A lot of possibilities here," he
said with exaggerated kindness, "but Lyme is definitely one
of them. I think you should try antibiotics again."

At this point in my paranoia and confusion, it felt as
though the earlier antibiotics had *caused* the phantom heart
attacks—that taking doxycycline without a positive Lyme
test had rolled me further down the spiral staircase. So although I dutifully acquired the bottle of pills—amoxicillin
this time, in case the doxycycline had really been too hard on
my stomach—I put them by my bedside and spent days ago-
nizing over whether I should take them.

One early-September night, we were supposed to go to a
party at my father's house. In my permanent fog, I had somehow overturned the Xanax bottle and left a pill or two lying
in fragments on the bedroom floor. Our two-year-old picked
one up and ate it. The ambulance came, the medics exam-
ined her, she was fine. But it was another pit that seemed to
open underneath my feet.

Long is the way and hard, that out of Hell leads up to light. I
had a poseur's knowledge of John Milton, a vague college
memory of *Paradise Lost*. But that line somehow reverberated
in my head.

I took the amoxicillin.

2

Controversy

I N 1956, A PAINTER AND NEWLYWED NAMED POLLY MUR-
ray moved with her husband from New York City to
Essex, Connecticut, a pleasant town that sits just a few miles
north of where the Connecticut River flows out into the
Long Island Sound. It's a landscape of wetlands and wood-
lands, dotted with antique stores and bed-and-breakfasts—
a perfect spot for tourists and weekenders, beautiful enough
to boast a painting school and artists' colony, an ideal place to
raise a family. The Murrays rented a small house, she took
sailing lessons, and soon she was pregnant with the first of
their four children. Early in the pregnancy she suddenly fell
ill, with aches and a fever and bleeding that almost cost her
the baby. After her son was born, the family moved across
the river, to a house with a bigger yard where they built a
rock garden, in another lovely little town called Lyme.

The illness from Murray's first pregnancy was repeated in
her later ones. She had angry red rashes, recurring sore
throats, pain in her chest. After the birth of her third child,
she began suffering excruciating headaches, shooting pains
in her legs, agony so intense it felt like her knee was popping from its joint. During her fourth pregnancy, a wide red

streak, raised and prickly like sandpaper, was mysteriously painted on her face. Her doctors diagnosed her with scoliosis, synovitis, pleurisy, erysipelas—a laundry list of obscure conditions tailored to the individual symptoms rather than the whole. But they also offered psychological explanations ("sometimes people subconsciously want to be sick," she was informed) and dismissed her as a "doctor chaser."

So the family lived with the mystery until her oldest sons were teenagers. Then both boys began to exhibit their own dramatic symptoms: headaches and recurring fevers, insomnia, stiffness in the extremities—and then swelling in their knees and ankles, which was diagnosed as juvenile rheumatoid arthritis.

At this point Murray noticed that there seemed to be a cluster of juvenile arthritis cases in her riverside neighborhood—a dozen or more local kids with the same rare diagnosis. Another local mother, Judith Mensch, had noticed the same thing, and the two mothers contacted the Connecticut Department of Health, which dispatched a young Yale rheumatologist named Allen Steere to investigate the cluster of cases—up to thirty-nine children by the time he got involved. Half of them lived on just four roads; most of them had fallen ill around the same time, in the summer and fall.

Steere was an unusual medical type, a former concert violinist, and he extended a sympathy to Murray and her neighbors that few prior experts had shown. With their help, he cataloged a raft of different symptoms in the cluster of cases, so diverse and general as to frustrate easy diagnosis. But his early work also yielded what seemed to be a common early signifier: the red target, the bull's-eye rash, a widening circle spreading from a tiny lesion, a papule on the skin.

This indicator, combined with the seasonality of the illness and the association with people who lived in the wooded estuary rather than the town centers, led Steere and his team to the truth: They were dealing with a sickness spread by the deer tick, an adaptable creature that piggybacks on chipmunks and mice and dogs and human beings as well as deer, and whose smallest forms—the springtime phases, larval and nymphal—are about the diameter of a poppyseed.

This was 1975, year zero for the American understanding of Lyme disease, four years before my birth. In Europe it had been identified earlier, likely by a Swedish dermatologist named Arvid Afzelius in the nineteenth century; by the late twentieth century it was understood to be a tick-borne spirochete capable of causing all manner of ills, including a chronic neurological illness dubbed Bannwarth syndrome.

The prehistory is more obscure. There is one reference to a tick-borne illness causing "exquisite pain" in "the interior parts of the limbs," by a naturalist visiting the isle of Jura, off Scotland's west coast, in the 1760s. An autopsy of "Ötzi the Iceman," a 5,300-year-old mummy preserved in the Swiss Alps, found the DNA of the Lyme spirochete in his tissue. But in the millennia separating Ötzi's demise from the naturalist's Jura trip, there are no clear accounts of Lyme disease in human records.

Some scientists have speculated that the disease arrived in North America with European colonists, perhaps carrying some of those dangerous Jura ticks. But the DNA-sleuthing work of biologists suggests that the spirochete was present in North America going back thousands of years at least, spreading via Native American human hosts from the Northeast to the Midwest, whose present-day strains of the disease diverge. It's possible that the rapid deforestation accomplished by New England farmers in the seventeenth and eighteenth centuries saved European settlers from an epidemic by wiping out enough tick habitats to confine the disease to a few pockets of deep forest. Then presumably it recovered somewhat with farm abandonment in the nineteenth century, when the people who worked the rocky soil around our dream house became frustrated with its meager fruits and headed west, leaving their pastures to be reclaimed by forest and their stone walls to picturesque decay. It spread farther as deer populations gradually recovered, and waited in the woods for the great trend of the mid-twentieth century, suburbanization, to deliver it a vast new population of unknowing human hosts.

That story has its difficulties, but it does a decent enough job of explaining the New England origins of the modern epidemic, the way it radiates like a rash from southern Connecticut, without requiring recourse to more conspiratorial accounts. (The biowarfare laboratory on Plum Island, in the Long Island Sound just south of the Connecticut River estuary, quickly became a locus of suspicion.) It also helps explain why Steere and his Yale colleagues were hesitant to simply pick up on preexisting European research, which advised the use of antibiotics for treatment, though nobody had yet identified the pathogen. Instead they thought they might be dealing with a genuinely novel epidemic, perhaps caused by a tick-borne virus rather than bacteria—in which case antibiotics would be useless.

Meanwhile, Steere's name for the disease soon caught on generally, so that today in France and Germany and Scandinavia, if you wake up with a rash from a tick bite, you will be diagnosed with a condition named for the shoreline of Connecticut, for the towns where white shingles and carefully mowed backyards meet the shadow of the woods.

. . .

Steere didn't just give Lyme a name, however. He also established a template for its treatment. Other Connecticut doctors who encountered the illness, including a pediatrician outside New Haven and a pair of Navy doctors at the submarine base in Groton, were doing what the European doctors did: They were prescribing antibiotics, usually penicillin, on the theory that some kind of bacterium was causing the affliction and you needed drugs to kill it. But Steere was a rheumatologist, accustomed to treating inflammations triggered by the body's own defenses. At the beginning, he treated his patients' symptoms with drugs designed to suppress inflammation and calm the immune system—aspirin in mild cases, steroids in more severe ones—while reserving judgment on whether it made sense to use antibiotics as well.

It took four years of trials—patients with the rash were given a week of penicillin in the summers of 1977 and 1979, but not in 1976 or 1978—to prove to his team's satisfaction that antibiotics seemed to be of some use, meaning that the infection was bacterial rather than viral. Then it took another four years for scientists to figure out what the antibiotics were actually killing. In 1982, a research scientist named Willy Burgdorfer, using blood samples sent to his laboratory from an outbreak on Long Island, finally identified the responsible bacterium—a spirochete, like syphilis, which takes its designation from its corkscrew shape. Today the bacterium bears his name, *Borrelia burgdorferi*.

But even with these discoveries, Steere and many of the doctors who came after him prescribed antibiotics only for people who actually had a bull's-eye present on their skin, and withheld them from patients dealing with the many symptoms that could follow. This group, they assumed, was no longer dealing with an active illness—an assumption confirmed by the many cases where taking a short course of antibiotics did not seem to help. Instead their condition was probably "post-infectious," a matter of an overtriggered immune system run amok—much like lupus, rheumatoid arthritis, and the other illnesses that rheumatologists were accustomed to treating. The problem had started with an infection, but now there was no invasion left to kill.

That was the more sympathetic perspective. To less sympathetic doctors, the array of weird symptoms claimed by Lyme patients and their duration long after an infection led to the same conclusion drawn by Polly Murray's doctors: Whatever the initial trigger, psychological problems and hypochondria had to be at work.

And the array really was astonishing. Throughout the 1980s, as cases multiplied in Connecticut and Long Island and then across the Northeast, researchers documented a wide diversity of Lyme symptoms, extending beyond pain and fatigue to encompass problems with just about every organ group, plus a battery of neurological problems: compulsions, depression, memory loss, neural degeneration that mimicked multiple sclerosis. The term "great imitator" had previously been applied to syphilis; now a doctor named Andrew Pachner dubbed Lyme the *new* great imitator, for the range of symptoms that its burrowing corkscrew could conjure from protesting human flesh.

Once conjured, they very often lingered: Not in the majority of Lyme cases, but in a substantial minority, up to 20 percent of sufferers, people either stayed sick, relapsed, or saw peculiar symptoms emerge later—as though the disease could be forced into hibernation, but there was always a chance that it would wake up.

The Murray family was a good example. In Polly Murray's memoir, written with a preternatural calm that was rare in the emerging Lyme debate, she described the various symptoms that dogged her and her children decades after Steere treated them. "As a family we have generally been lucky," she insisted, but her family's "luck" encompassed descriptions like this one, applied to her youngest son: "In the years following this episode Todd has been feeling well, with the exceptions of periods of insomnia, recurrent uncontrollable muscle twitching, occasional joint pain, and a sun rash he has had intermittently since he first developed Lyme disease." Along with these kinds of recurring symptoms, everyone in her family, including her now ex-husband, had heart issues, arrhythmias, and fibrillations, years after their Lyme diagnosis—which couldn't definitively be traced to their original illness, but tracked with the experiences of other chronic sufferers.

Still, Murray and her family members were definitely lucky in one sense: They found doctors who prescribed antibiotics consistently whenever they relapsed, which, "when given for long enough," she recorded, usually helped symptoms to abate. Many chronic or relapsing patients weren't so fortunate. They would have to hunt to find doctors who would go further than Steere and the emerging consensus, doctors who would treat patients whose symptoms lingered for longer periods, with multiple antibiotics and an approach that varied with each case.

The chronic Lyme patients also found themselves grouped together with other illnesses with mysterious causes that were coming into the public consciousness at the time. Fibromyalgia, a catchall description of recurring pain symptoms without a certain cause, first showed up in *The Journal of the American Medical Association* in 1987. Chronic fatigue syndrome, which often seemed to take hold in the wake of the commonplace Epstein-Barr virus, was first defined by the Centers for Disease Control in 1988. Multiple chemical sensitivity, a much-debated term for people with strong reactions to perfumes, pesticides, plastics, and other accoutrements of modern life, came into common use around the same time; it was a diagnosis my mother was given when I was young. After 1991, so-called Gulf War syndrome added the specific suffering of veterans to the list of contested, poorly understood forms of chronic sickness.

Reasonably enough, people assumed that there were probably some commonalities among these conditions, which enveloped hundreds of thousands and then millions of Americans during the 1990s and 2000s, delivering them to pain and depression and isolation and helping to set the stage for the rise of middle-age drug abuse and suicide in the 2010s.

Somewhat less reasonably, the medical system decided that the best explanation for most of these afflictions was either the "post-infection" theory, where the problem was all in the suffering person's malfunctioning immune system, or else some more mysterious and psychosomatic problem, some vulnerability of the psyche rather than the flesh.

Meanwhile, only on the margins was there discussion of the connections between Lyme infections and other seemingly incurable conditions. (In 1987, a Long Island pathologist turned Lyme researcher published a study in *Human Pathology* of four frozen brains from deceased Alzheimer's patients: In all four, the brain plaques that are a hallmark of the disease were suffused with Lyme spirochetes. There was no follow-up until the subsequent decade.) And only a few Lyme researchers were interested in the stranger features of the spirochetes, which Burgdorfer's research had stressed—their shape-shifting quality, the way their spirals could change into hooks and balls and strings and weirder shapes, and even seemingly grow hardened cyst-like walls. In the test tube, the transformations often happened when they were exposed to antibiotics—as though the spirochetes registered danger and shape-shifted in self-defense.

THE CONSENSUS AROUND LYME DISEASE WAS SEALED IN 1991, when there were enough new reported cases—ten thousand and climbing—for the Centers for Disease Control to begin national surveillance for Lyme, establish formal diagnostic criteria, and endorse a two-tier testing regimen: the ELISA test followed by the Western blot, two different ways of looking for Lyme antibodies in the patient's blood.

Diagnostic standardization was supposed to establish a consistent baseline for national case reporting, not rule out the possibility of atypical cases or constrain doctors from diagnosing them. But in practice it did exactly that, narrowing the range of cases that counted as "real" Lyme by encouraging doctors to limit their diagnoses to a CDC-approved set of symptoms, mostly visible manifestations like joint swelling and the famous rash. Meanwhile, the testing rules had a similar effect: The two-tier approach reduced the risk of false positives, but it created a larger chance of false negatives, missing anywhere from a third to half of early Lyme cases, and as many as 25 percent of cases even in late-stage, neurologic Lyme.

The incentive structures forged by the CDC were a fascinating case study in how bureaucracy shapes science as much as the other way around, how without any conscious decision, let alone conspiracy, scientific research can end up pushed again and again down the same well-worn tracks. The narrow diagnostic criteria became the benchmark not just for doctors treating patients but for researchers when they applied for public grants, so that Lyme research increasingly focused on only the most certain diagnoses and left all ambiguous cases and potential false negatives alone. This approach ratified the establishment's confidence in their own rules of evidence: A study might show that most Lyme patients had the typical presentations (clear blood tests, consistent early symptoms) . . . but only after making one or more of these presentations a prerequisite for being admitted to the study in the first place.

Likewise, after 1991, insurance companies began to deny payment for Lyme cases that didn't meet the CDC criteria. If you were a doctor who wanted to diagnose or treat more broadly, you basically had to become a medical outsider— a maverick, the sort of weird specialist who didn't take insurance, who risked scrutiny from state medical boards, and so on down a list of attributes that self-selected for eccentricity, stubbornness, and a touch of crankery.

So the CDC guidelines essentially ratified the split already opening in the 1980s, between an official understanding of the disease and a dissenting view, between a medical establishment that felt satisfied with how it diagnosed and treated this novel-seeming pathogen and a growing population of patients and sufferers (or self-described sufferers, at least) who felt ignored, abandoned, and betrayed. It created not just two worldviews but two cultures, two concentric circles of insiders and outsiders—the inner one confident and authoritative and buoyed by institutional support, the outer one more fluid and open-minded but also necessarily more peculiar and paranoid and sometimes, frankly, gonzo in its theories and experiments. There were even two different medical associations—the Infectious Diseases Society of America issued the mainstream guidelines, while the dissenters formed the International Lyme and Associated Diseases Society, which issued recommendations of its own.

Through it all, Allen Steere's initial assumption—that long-term symptoms from the disease simply couldn't be caused by the bacterium itself, and therefore couldn't be usefully treated with antibiotics—remained the first culture's orthodoxy, creating a larger and larger pool of people who were told that their struggles weren't Lyme disease, or had been Lyme disease and weren't anymore, or, in some sense, were only in their heads.

There were harsher and kinder ways of offering this last assessment. The sneering version ran in the *Annals of Internal Medicine* in 1991, the same year the CDC handed down its guidelines. It was a humor column, so-called, by one Ludwig Lettau, M.D., who wrote as an expert for the "Centers for Fatigue Control" to describe a spreading epidemic of "Lime disease"—distinguished from true Lyme, he wrote, by its concentration among upper-middle-class women, its "weak to moderate association with previous attendance at cocktail parties serving lime-garnished mixed drinks," and its "very strong association with recent exposure to media stories on Lyme disease."

The gentler approach belonged to Steere himself, who

became over these years a target for the rage of sick people who felt betrayed or abandoned by the establishment. In 2001, David Grann profiled him for *The New York Times Magazine,* in a piece entitled "Stalking Dr. Steere," with an arresting opening line: "Last year, Dr. Allen Steere, one of the world's most renowned medical researchers and rheumatologists, began to fear patients." Not his own, but the ones he wouldn't treat, the ones he thought wouldn't be helped by antibiotics.

Grann described the dangerous extremes that some of these unbalanced sufferers had reached: how what began with letters begging Steere for help had escalated to a constant drumbeat of harassment, death threats, protests at his public appearances, and bomb scares. All of it was driven by a campaign of online vilification from patients who depicted him "as a demon, worse than the spirochetes . . . that they claimed inhabited their bodies."

The article portrayed Steere's position as tragic, the man of science unable to prevent his discovery from legitimizing the creation of a "parallel universe" outside the normal realms of medicine—"a universe in which there were now hundreds of Polly Murrays, self-taught medical experts armed with their own doctors and research."

At one point in the story, Steere read aloud a letter from one of these self-taught sufferers, which listed dozens of symptoms "on the back page in neat shaky letters." It was a nightmarish concatenation—"severe fatigue, muscle pain, low-grade fevers, intolerance to heat or cold, hot flashes, weight gain, weight loss, numbness and tingling in skull and limbs, seeing black spots, sinus infections, constant infections, palpitations, severe digestive disorder, high-pitch ringing in both ears, leg jerks, poor sleeping habits, food allergies, severely altered balance, mood swings, deteriorating handwriting"— that seemed too wild and broad to follow from the disease that he helped discover:

> Steere put down the letter and stared at me for a long moment. "What I suspect is that she doesn't have Lyme disease but some kind of psychiatric illness," he said. He paused, as if already anticipating the impact of his words. "That does not mean I don't care about her or what happens to her."

But you can't treat someone, in good conscience, for a disease you don't believe they have.

I WAS IN COLLEGE WHEN THE STEERE PROFILE RAN, AND I have the dimmest memory of reading it. But his assumptions I knew well, because they defined the understanding of Lyme disease that I absorbed as a teenager, growing up in a state shadowed by the illness, with warnings from camp counselors and tick checks on summer hiking programs and a run of Lyme stories in the newspaper headlines every spring.

Under its premises, Lyme was serious but usually not *that* serious. If you were bitten by a tick, you had to watch out for the bull's-eye (in my wife's Connecticut childhood, she and her sister used to use a suction cup to press circles into their legs to frighten their mother), and if you missed it you could expect flu-like symptoms: fevers and headaches and chills. If the disease wasn't diagnosed then, there was the possibility of really serious problems like arthritis down the road.

So, all in all, a potentially dangerous infection—but one whose arrival was usually branded on your skin, whose offensives could be halted and rolled back easily at the early stages, and which turned devastating only if you missed months and months of signs. A few of Abby's classmates had this happen, but even then, a PICC line and a flood of IV antibiotics seemed to suffice for a return to normal. Maybe you'd have to miss a few weeks of school, like the kids who came down with mono, and maybe you'd have vague aches and pains thereafter, but that would be an extraordinary case. In Abby's high school, the older kids referred to the feeling of a bad hangover as "Lymie legs," suggesting that the illness was no more to be feared than the rough comedown from a particularly outrageous bender.

In my own childhood, I had no direct experience of Lyme. We found ticks on our legs now and then; once, at least, I remember my mother using the heat from a match to coax an engorged deer tick out from underneath my skin. But I was never sick, none of my friends were ever seriously ill, and it wasn't until I had left Connecticut for Washington, D.C., that we had a closer brush with the dark things that the tiny bugs can carry.

The occasion was the death of my grandfather's second wife, a California transplant named Lyn whose watercolors had become a sort of family business, run out of their shared farmhouse on the Maine coast, where her flower gardens blended into the wildflowers that edged the saltwater woodland around their home. Suddenly, in her seventies, she passed into a coma, a mysterious collapse that was traced after her death to a rare infection called the Powassan virus, a tick-borne illness that kills 10 percent of those infected. There were thirty-three cases in the United States between 2001 and 2010; my step-grandmother was one of a handful of deaths.

This was a horrifying turn of events, a reason to keep out of the woods around my grandfather's farmhouse, and eventually to keep my toddling kids off even the lawn where I'd once played in the summers. But as it related to Lyme disease, Lyn's death mostly seemed like another reason to minimize the significance and severity of the much more common tick-borne illness. After all, having had a family encounter with a *real* tick-borne killer, I thought I knew something about what actual devastation looked like. The threat of a rash and fever and some sort of aches and pains thereafter seemed like little or nothing by comparison.

But the truth was that even after Lyn's bizarre death, even as Abby and I fixated on the Connecticut countryside, I barely thought about ticks at all. Nobody likes to focus on the dark things in the corners of their dreamworlds; nobody who fantasizes about a tropical beach house wants to think about the sharks.

I certainly didn't pay close attention to the persistence of the Lyme controversy, which had two notable turning points in the years between my leaving Connecticut and our not-so-triumphant return. First, around the same time as the Steere profile, there were three large-scale trials, funded by the National Institutes of Health, of longer-term intravenous antibiotic treatments for patients who had persistent Lyme symptoms. The first two trials showed no improvement whatsoever; the third showed improvement in fatigue but not in other symptoms. While that result implied that there might be some benefit to extended treatment, the authors still recommended against long-term antibiotics, given the risks of IV treatment and the relatively limited improvement.

Taken together, the studies helped solidify medical confidence in the official approach, the short courses of antibiotics, and further marginalize the dissenters.

Then, beginning in 2008, there was another shift, kicked off by a study demonstrating that a Lyme infection could persist in mammals even after antibiotic treatment. The study had a fascinating design: Instead of testing its mouse subjects for Lyme antibodies after treatment, the authors let a laboratory-raised tick, free of *Borrelia,* feed on the supposedly cured mouse. The tick didn't just suck up blood; it sucked up spirochetes. The disease was still in there.

Other studies followed, on beagles and macaques as well as mice, and soon there was a weighty amount of evidence for Lyme's persistence after the kind of limited duration that the CDC recommended for antibiotic treatment, and that most doctors prescribed. This gave new ammunition to the dissidents and their patients and summoned forth new rounds of research. So did the fact that during these years, Lyme disease was spreading rapidly—a trend variously blamed on climate change (warm winters are good for ticks) and the continued growth of sprawl. It had been a Connecticut and Long Island epidemic initially, then a New England and New Jersey and Hudson Valley epidemic. By the 2010s a map of reported cases darkened the whole Northeast and shadowed eastern Ohio, the upper South, and parts of Florida, with a separate speckling for the Upper Midwest and California. The CDC estimated 117,000 new cases in 1995; by 2015, the year we moved back to Connecticut, the number was up to 380,000; by 2019 it was 476,000.

The best book yet written about Lyme disease (which I have pillaged in writing this chapter) was also published around this time. Entitled *Cure Unknown,* it was the work of

Pamela Weintraub, a science journalist who moved with her husband and two sons to a verdant Westchester town much like the one in which my wife and I had bought our country manse. Then they all fell ill, in different ways (one son was carried under by sickness after a day spent playing in leaf piles) that defied the mainstream Westchester doctors' wisdom. Eventually the family members were all diagnosed with tick-borne illnesses, found their way to the more eccentric Lyme-literate doctors, and very gradually got better, but with countless false starts and twists and turns along the way. And Weintraub, in a truly heroic effort, managed to research and report the first comprehensive history of the Lyme controversy at the same time that she was trying to save her sons, her husband, and herself. (One small but telling thing she did was find the woman who had sent Allen Steere that insane-sounding letter; she was perfectly sane and had tested positive for Lyme.)

Out of all these influences, the 2010s brought a notable change in the way Lyme disease was covered in the press. When the *Times Magazine* profiled Steere in 2001, the stress was heavily on the scientific consensus and the threat from its self-taught enemies. But when *The New Yorker*'s Michael Specter covered the "Lyme Wars" in 2013, the stress was more on the patients failed by the official view, their testimonials of being helped by the dissenting doctors, and the struggles of the establishment experts he interviewed to explain away the evidence for Lyme's persistence.

But all these developments still didn't change the fundamental order of the Lyme-treatment universe. If the disease itself was intractable, so was the argument over its treatment, the two concentric circles of debate. The doctors who defended the established view conceded that some bacteria might survive in certain patients' systems. But the mere presence of such "persisters" didn't prove that the bugs—as opposed to immune-system problems or psychological disturbances—were what caused the continuing suffering and symptoms. Even if sometimes bacteria were (maybe!) responsible for (some, a few!) chronic cases, the dissenters were offering not one alternative to the official approach to treatment but a wide and shifting range of possibilities, none of which had a double-blind placebo-controlled study to back them up. And the dissenting approaches were hardly risk-free: At an individual level, antibiotics often have side effects, and IV antibiotics carry extra perils; at the level of the larger population, overprescribing antibiotics can create drug-resistant superbugs. So just under normal medical assumptions, the establishment voices argued, the limited-antibiotic regimen remained the only reasonable choice.

THEY CONTINUED TO WIN THIS ARGUMENT IN PART BECAUSE, despite all the cracks in the consensus, the world of chronic-Lyme treatment remained so eccentric and outré. When a reporter named Molly Fischer wrote about the culture of chronic Lyme for *New York* magazine in 2019, she visited two outposts of the Lyme treatment world. On the one hand, there was the chronic-Lyme specialist in New York City, a confident elder statesman with a "rakish goatee," charging thousands of dollars for his complex treatment protocols of antibiotics and herbal remedies and confidently explaining to the doubtful reporter that his medical instincts could identify Lyme cases even when the blood tests were ambiguous. At the time of the interview, he was "on a three-year probation with the New York State Board for Professional Medical

Conduct," she noted, "over allegations that include gross negligence, gross incompetence, and failure to maintain adequate medical records."

Fischer's other outpost was the Lyme support group she visited, somewhere deep in the suburbs, led by a Reiki master who affirmed all the various complicated stories that the attendees unfolded—some of them resembling the wild letters that Steere had sighed over regretfully two decades earlier—and then promised that her methods of energetic healing could help them all recover, as they had helped her recover once upon a time. And all at a far cheaper price than what the big-city doctors were offering: "Energy healing provided techniques to try on your own, no doctor's appointment required," and "if any of them wanted to come in for a session, she told them, she could give them 50 percent off her usual rate of $250."

After these forays into claustrophobic-seeming worlds, you could sense Fischer returning with a kind of relief to the mainstream experts, who dismissed the strange landscape of chronic treatment in soothing, reasonable tones—tones that promised that the world is comprehensible, that modern medicine knows what it's doing, that anyone too far outside the system is either seduced by pseudoscience or culpably exploiting people.

That was where the debate on chronic Lyme disease stood at the time I was taken ill—with "first, do no harm" still being the mainstream-medical justification for doing little or nothing for many thousands of sick people.

If you had Lyme-like symptoms and circumstances but a negative test result, you might be able to talk your way into a short trial of antibiotics—as I did in D.C.—but officially you belonged to the growing American population of the

mysteriously ill, who could be offered sleep aids and antidepressants but nothing that would actually fight an infection.

If you were a positive case with lingering, persistent symptoms after treatment, then your Lyme officially belonged to
the past, and you no longer had a CDC-recognized disease.
Instead you had something called Post-Treatment Lyme Disease Syndrome (PTLDS), and the CDC's advice for anyone
suffering through it was to basically keep on suffering, because
"long-term antibiotic treatment for Lyme disease has been associated with serious, sometimes deadly complications," and
a regimen of patience and optimism was the better course:
"Patients with PTLDS usually get better over time, but it can
take many months to feel completely well."

In the meantime you would be offered . . . nothing. No
treatments, no openness to experiments, just sympathy joined
to a confidence that the most important thing was to not risk
doing any extra harm.

So after forty-six years of controversy, for anyone with
Lyme or a Lyme-like illness who remains miserably sick
months or years later, the official, expert-approved, inner-
circle view remains at one with the diagnosis offered by the
doctors who initially treated Polly Murray, a diagnosis at
once extremely simple and extremely strange:

You have a disease that does not exist.

3

The Secret of the Suburbs

I TOOK THE ANTIBIOTIC, AND AGAIN, AS WITH THE DOXY-cycline two months earlier, the pain inside me changed. A flood across my shoulders, a knocking in my knees. I stalked our empty new house late at night, the soles of my feet burning and my spine aflame. I woke up in the mornings feeling like I had been beaten by a boxer overnight.

But I *woke* up, from a sleep that was brief and poor but still actual sleep, four or five hours instead of the hour that I had been getting since July. And the feeling of physical dissociation, perpetual almost-dizziness, of half my body being disconnected from the other, was gone after a week on the amoxicillin.

Those were dramatic changes, worth the surge of pain, and they made me think anew that it really was Lyme or some other infection, since literally nothing else I tried had given me anything back that I had lost.

By this time I had two recommendations for Lyme specialists, both from my father's New York friend who researched the disease. Both were supposed to be more aggressive than the official CDC consensus dictated, and though I had no definite view on the Lyme debate as yet, I did not feel as though I was likely to be better after three weeks of treatment. (Indeed, I had already taken almost a two-week course in my earlier, haphazard doxycycline trial.) So "aggressive" seemed like what I wanted.

The first doctor had a basement office on the Upper East Side, a piece of tape across his nose, and an avuncular, reassuring manner. Yes, he said, I probably had Lyme—the symptoms fit, the boil was probably a bite, the blood tests missed lots of cases, he saw people like me all the time. But no, I didn't need to worry that much about the disastrous chronic cases I was now reading about obsessively on the internet. Those were mostly people who had something else wrong with them, who were infirm or obese or mentally disturbed, and I was young and previously healthy and likely to be fine.

The truth, as this doctor saw it—I'll call him the Reassurer—was somewhere between the establishment view and the fullness of dissent. Lots of Lyme cases, especially well-entrenched Lyme cases, took more than a few weeks to clear, and he usually prescribed antibiotics for a few months. But that would be enough, he promised: I would be much, much better by Thanksgiving, and well within a year.

The second doctor was something else entirely. He had a wood-paneled office one town over from our new house, more like a den than a clinic, and books and pamphlets littering the waiting room, each seeming to offer a different theory on how one might treat an entrenched case of Lyme. One book was nothing but patient testimonials, people describing how the disease had changed their lives; in my parlous state it was harrowing to read.

The doctor himself looked a bit like a forest creature,

with a trim build and rounded cheeks that protruded slightly, like a squirrel with a nut or two socked away inside. He talked to me for ninety minutes, took copious notes, asked a thousand questions, and revealed himself to be a true dissenter, a total maverick. Chronic Lyme was an epidemic, he said, wildly underdiagnosed and totally mistreated, its victims fed a pack of lies about the non-persistence of the disease by doctors too invested in their paradigm to accept the obvious evidence around them. He had been fighting this battle for fifteen years, getting hundreds if not thousands of patients better along the way. Could he get me better? Probably, but I was obviously very sick, and it would take a while. Most of his patients took high doses of antibiotics for around a year; I might need more; some needed years and years of treatment.

This seemed like too much. The Reassurer offered a plausible balancing of ideas, a reasonable synthesis; the Maverick just frightened me. Even if I felt I had already tested its limits, I still wanted to believe in the medical consensus. So I followed the Reassurer's advice, raised the dose of amoxicillin, and settled in to await the recovery he promised.

At times that fall I thought it was happening. For four months I took the antibiotics, and I frequently experienced something like the "Herxheimers" that were described by Lyme sufferers online: the increase in symptoms, supposedly caused by dying spirochetes, that was usually followed by a feeling of weakness and exhaustion, sometimes with a panting thirst or a craving appetite. There was often an all-but-irresistible urge to move the affected portion of my body, to pinwheel my arms or stomp my feet, to tense and squeeze my stomach, to thrust my hips like a lewd automaton, or to rub furiously at whatever place the pain was burning. When the pain subsided, a horrible itch would often take its place. I would go in the shower after taking an antibiotic and come out streaked bright red from frantic scratching.

All this seemed like it might be part of the cure, the bacteria getting killed and flushed out of my system in a debilitating cascade. I would sometimes feel a little better for an hour out of a day, or a day out of a week, and when I did, my mind would leap ahead happily to wellness, to the comfortable life we had been planning, to the essay I would write about the whole interesting experience—"My Summer of Lyme" or some such, a fascinating medical mystery with a happy resolution.

But the feeling-better moments never held, and I kept falling back into the pain and dark.

I was able to travel for speaking a little bit, part of the normal columnist job, but the variation in my experience was sharp. I flew to Notre Dame in late September and in the Westchester airport ran into a Benedictine monk, young and fiercely bearded, whom I had met the previous spring. He was headed somewhere else entirely but on the flight to Chicago with me. The first thing I said to him was "I dreamed about you." (I had—very strangely—a week earlier.) The second thing I did was sob. (There was a lot of sobbing in those days.)

He handled it with monkish equanimity, praying with me there in a corner of the tiny commuter airport between the newsstand and the metal detectors, and giving me the hardest-core Catholic advice on suffering. "It's a gift," he said flatly. "It's not something to just wish away or run from. It's there for purgation, refinement, redirection if you've wandered onto the wrong path. And if you're on the right path,

doing important work"—a soft smile behind the beard—
"well, then you should expect to get some demonic attacks
from time to time."

When we parted after the flight to Chicago, I watched his
brown habit vanish into the greens and blues of the O'Hare
crowds, and then I went on to South Bend, where for the
rest of the trip I felt different, better, like I was gaining ground
as I walked around the campus and prayed under the golden
dome. Flying home, I told myself that the encounter with
the Benedictine had been the turning point, the divine land-
mark on the journey back into the light.

And naturally, the part of the monk's advice that my none-
too-stable mind really latched on to was the part about doing
important work, rather than the part about being chastised
or redirected. As a writer in those months, I was embroiled
in the beginnings of the intra-conservative battle over Donald Trump, the attempts to rally opposition to his candidacy,
and also in arguments within the Catholic Church, the rising
debates over divorce and remarriage under Pope Francis.
These were more significant-seeming dramas than the Obama-
era controversies I was used to writing about, but maybe they
were even more significant than I understood. Maybe I had
some actual historical part to play from my unique paper-of-
record perch. Maybe I just had to get through this sickness,
this *attack,* and then—from the security of our rural retreat—
I could do the work that I was meant to do.

These bouts of grandiosity offered little succor when the
trips later in the fall were worse. I drove to Syracuse a few
weeks into October, the peak of autumn color, and pulled
over every hour to stomp around a rest stop or gag into a
toilet. I flew to D.C., my first time back, for a think-tank

panel, and my legs shook below the table and my forehead poured sweat. Afterward I had lunch with an old colleague and startled the sushi-goers with my sobs.

In November I gave a talk in New York that was supposed to be about the state of the Catholic Church, but somehow I broke away from the main theme midway through to talk about my sickness and I almost began crying on the stage. There was a storm of sympathetic applause when I finished, but the kindness afterward was painful, mixing platitudes with the kinds of stories I didn't want to hear, about friends and family members who had Lyme or something like Lyme and had taken years to get better, or weren't well even now.

"Do you have a good protocol?" one older woman said to me after talking for a while about her afflicted son. I didn't know exactly what "protocol" meant, but I knew it was some kind of Lyme lingo for the combinations that the more extreme doctors used, doctors like the Maverick, doctors whose help I didn't want to believe I needed, because I was going to be all fixed up by Thanksgiving.

"You really need to find the protocol that works for you," she said, her hand gripping mine, liver spots against my burning skin, and I said something vaguely agreeable and escaped to the bathroom for a round of gagging in a stall.

The clarifying trip took me to Harvard sometime in November. The event itself went well enough, though my legs wobbled and I had a wave of prickling all over my head while I sat under the vault of Annenberg Hall, listening to the aged sociologist Peter Berger talking wisely about secularism. But early the next morning I woke in the hotel with a burning sensation all around my throat, and I went to the mirror and saw that my entire upper torso was as red as a

Soviet banner. Then I felt the old summertime pressure on my chest, the horrible closing-up feeling in my throat, and I was sure that I was going to die there, alone in a hotel room. I called the front desk, gagging, and begged for an ambulance. As I waited for it to come, I prayed and scrolled through pictures of my kids, the fear that I would leave them fatherless returning in a rush.

Of course by the time they carried me out of that hotel on a stretcher and took me to the ER for tests, the pain had subsided and I was breathing normally again. Of course the tests they did were all normal; of course the doctors listened to my explanations with a mix of puzzlement and pity. On the train back to Connecticut, there was a brief recurrence, another unnerving throat tightening as the train rattled through Rhode Island—but then it passed and I was back to a more bearable sort of pain.

But with it came a new, definite knowledge. Whatever the antibiotics were doing for me, I was still returning to the same places, still circling through the same pointless ER trips. Sitting on the train as the Connecticut coastline rushed past on the left—the wintry wetlands and shore towns, New London, Old Saybrook, Lyme—I accepted that the Reassurer had been wrong in his confident predictions, that I wasn't really getting better. At this rate, if there was a rate, I would be sick for fifty years, sick until I died.

THE ARGUMENT THAT LYME DISEASE CAN PERSIST, DEVASTATingly, despite antibiotic treatment is not bizarre or esoteric. It requires no New Age mysticism, no fringe assumptions, no unusual theories of disease. It begins with patient experience, and a straightforward reading of the anecdata of Lyme victims. If someone has an illness, takes a drug to treat it, and afterward retains exactly the same symptoms, why wouldn't you assume that they have simply continued to have the same disease? Why invent a mysterious "post-disease syndrome" to explain what is experienced by the patient as one continuous sickness?

Especially since it's clear from the medical evidence that *Borrelia* is a special beast, and a good candidate to take a chronic form. It's a partial immunosuppressant, a precondition for establishing chronic infection. It's a penetrative bacterium, pushing into cells and burying itself in connective tissue, where fewer antibodies circulate and high antibiotic concentrations are harder to achieve. It's a survivor, with spirochetes persisting in petri dishes even after a supposedly killing dosage of antibiotics. Finally, the point that Willy Burgdorfer and others raised in the 1980s, peering at slides of spirochete-infected tissues, has been confirmed consistently since: *Borrelia* is a shape-shifter, taking on a hardened, defensive "cystic" form in the presence of antibiotics rather than its usual spiral, and possibly converting back to the more active form once the dose recedes.

Add all of this to the now-undisputed facts that the bacteria can survive substantial antibiotic treatment in nonhuman animals as well as test tubes, and the persistence of Lyme in human beings doesn't seem remotely surprising, or require any kind of autoimmune or psychosomatic hypothesis to explain.

By the middle of the fall I knew all of this from my obsessive reading, which joined with my persistent symptoms to wear away my crumbling hope that I would be an easy, consensus-vindicating case. But I was aware, too, that the skeptics of chronic Lyme had one strong arrow in their quiver: the fact that once you accept the persistence hypothesis, the question then becomes what to do about it—and the dissenters don't have a single simple answer.

Treating for more than a few weeks is the baseline, but it's also just the beginning. The Lyme specialists generally recommend bespoke combinations of antibiotics, "cocktails" that include intracellular drugs, drugs more likely to pass the blood-brain barrier, and more. Some recommend so-called pulsing, where antibiotics are administered in a two-week-on, two-week-off pattern, in the hope that the bacteria will essentially come out of hiding during the two weeks off, returning to the bloodstream and reproducing and thus making them easier to kill in the next antibiotic wave. Others suggest drugs and herbs that are supposed to work as "cyst busters," forcing *Borrelia* to morph back into a form that's more easily destroyed. Still others argue that the key to the bacteria's persistence is the formation of biofilms, complex bacterial colonies that are more antibiotic resistant than a free-floating pathogen; here, too, there are herbs and enzymes that are supposed to dissolve the biofilms, making it easier for either drugs or the immune system to kill the bacteria within.

Then, too, someone sick with Lyme may need to be treated for coinfections: other pathogens carried by the ticks, like the Powassan virus that killed my step-grandmother but much more commonplace, each with its own distinctive set of symptoms and potential treatments. There are so many of these—babesiosis, ehrlichiosis, spotted fever, bartonellosis, and more—that it might make sense to refer to the suite of tick-borne illnesses as "Lyme plus," the term that Steven Phillips and Dana Parish use in their recent book *Chronic,* one of the best distillations of chronic-Lyme theory and the treatment approaches it implies.

Because every patient is different, every strain of *Borrelia* and every mix of coinfections distinct, doctors urge sicker patients to embrace a medical version of FDR's "bold, persistent experimentation," adding dietary changes and herbal regimens and Epsom salt baths and all kinds of supplements to whatever mix of antibiotics they prescribe—creating personalized strategies, those *protocols* the old woman had spoken so insistently about. The dissenting view is that treatment for chronic Lyme isn't just a battle, but a long and grueling war.

THIS WAS THE KIND OF REGIMEN TO WHICH I DECIDED TO submit in the winter of 2016, as Trump began his march through the Republican primaries and Abby tried to finish editing her book and decorate a nursery before her due date. In December I let the Reassurer change my prescription from the amoxicillin to a more aggressive combination he sometimes used. My symptoms shifted somewhat, but after a month I was no better, and by now I didn't find the Reassurer particularly reassuring: I noticed that he told the same stories at every visit, cited the same cases, showed me the same picture of an athlete he had treated whose shoulder had been wrecked by Lyme. So in January I went back to the Maverick, accepted that I was leaving the CDC consensus decisively behind, and let him add another antibiotic to the course, with the promise that we might soon switch to a different three-drug combination.

The first few weeks on his regimen opened up new frontiers of pain, as though the medication had awakened, or reached into, regions of infection of which I had been mercifully unaware. The January night before our third child was born, I lay beside my wife with ice picks stabbing into my hips. The next day, while my newborn son lay pink and squalling under the nurses' care, and while Abby's epidural wore off and her own pain was rushing in, I was . . . well, not what I should have been, not a father caught up in wonder and appreciation, not a prop and a support, but a man unable to feel anything except the red-hot poker that seemed to be going directly through my chest.

I stood over my son as he lay in the incubator, the nurses murmuring and fussing around him, hoping that my performance was working and that I seemed like a normal enough dad . . . and then I had a vision of this experience extending forward, his scrunched-up eyes opening, his infancy and then his boyhood flowering, and through it all his father unable to be the dad he needed, not a baseball coach or a biking tutor but a cripple in the house, tapping away on columns to pay the bills, a shadow of the parent he deserved.

"Do you want to take him?" the nurse said. I held him to my chest, just where the pain was worst, pulling his natural warmth against my blazing fire.

But after this initial blast there was, mercifully, a span of marginal improvement. I still experienced the first days of my son's life like someone trapped inside a cloven pine, watching the rest of my family have normal experiences—normal joy, normal exhaustion—that were beyond my ability to feel. But if I was a robot I was at least a working one, capable of carrying and lullabying and driving out to get Abby bowls of Vietnamese broth: a father in function if not in full.

The stabilization encouraged the Maverick to have me

begin to pulse the antibiotics, two weeks on and two weeks off. The first time I went off the drugs was challenging but about what I expected. The pain diminished slightly, but the old dissociative feeling returned, and I felt weaker, more in danger of disintegration, with some of the old problems falling asleep. I survived two weeks like this and took the antibiotics again, which produced the expected new round of "herxing," as Lyme patients call the Herxheimer reaction, the pain and thirst and bouts of midday sleep.

Feeling faintly hopeful in the process, I went off the drugs again for my second pulse. This time the wave of returning symptoms was too much. I felt like a vise was constantly half-closed around my shoulders and my chest, just one turn of the screw away from crushing me. It was technically less painful than what happened when I took the Maverick's combination, but also proof that there are feelings worse than naked pain. I lasted forty-eight hours in this condition before returning to my antibiotics. The Herxheimer that followed had me throwing up all night and sleeping most of the following day.

There were men working outside while I vomited within. We had turned the multiplying outdoor projects on our property over to a soft-spoken, diminutive jack-of-all-trades named Luis, whom Abby had encountered building an endless stone wall in a nearby subdivision. We'd hired him after realizing that every other contractor made their bids on the unwise assumption that we were rich enough to afford the house we owned. "How you doing, Mr. Ross?" he would say to me when I came outside, pretending to oversee their efforts—the repairs to a cracking brick patio, the digging out of dying bushes, the tunneling for a curtain drain to clear away the floods that surged along the roadward side of the house whenever there were heavy rains.

The answer was "Not great," or even "Pretty desperate." Abby and I were increasingly locked into a pattern where we traded roles as I went up and down the roller coaster. She was stalwart and heroic while I went through my worst episodes, my failed pulses and surging Herxheimers—encouraging me in my despair while handling the kids and going over her book's copyedits and talking cheerfully to the grandparents or whatever personnel had shown up to work on the property that day. But then, once I had recovered a little bit, once I was able to repair the facade of normalcy and even feign a little of my old cheerfulness, the enormity of our situation came crashing down on her. Now it was her turn to be overwhelmed with emotion, to lie awake for hours, to contemplate our prospects with despair. At best you could say that we were taking turns holding each other up, but really it felt otherwise—more like our marriage was a leaky boat and we were taking turns filling it with water.

Our girls were somewhat protected from all this. They had school and grandparents, a big house to roam in, and each other as playmates, and they were young enough—or so I told myself in my optimistic, *I'm going to eventually get better* moments—that the memory of this experience would eventually fade. But at the same time, they sometimes seemed like sponges, absorbing our unhappiness even when we thought we were confining it to late-night arguments and tearful private conversations. More than once they woke up from nightmares that had somehow slipped from our bedroom into theirs.

Meanwhile, our baby claimed what little sleep I had regained, there were always new expenses on the property, and my ability to earn beyond my salary felt increasingly curtailed. The overgrown land around us, in which I had imagined our kids roaming happily, was now a dark territory, a landscape of peril. I forbade the girls to play beyond a narrow strip of upper lawn. I fantasized about shooting the deer that loped, uncaring, across our pasture.

We didn't meet our neighbors. Apart from our parents and the circulating handymen, we lived like hermits much of the time, and when we socialized all I could talk about was Lyme. I raved about it like a hysteric, or so it felt, but the reception was not what I expected: In context after context, from our church to our school to more random encounters across the town and state, the revelation of my illness was like a secret handshake or a pass code that opened up similar revelations about somebody's wife or son or neighbor. It wasn't just that everyone in that part of Connecticut had a Lyme story; it was that almost everyone had a chronic-Lyme story, almost everyone took it for granted that the medical consensus was wrong, almost everyone knew that treatment required someone like my doctor, and patience, and a bloody long time. *It took her two years to get better . . . He kept having relapses . . . She's never really recovered . . . I've just never been the same.*

Abby went to the playground with our kids on our first week after the move, and the very first parent she spoke to was planning to move out of the area because of a chronic-Lyme experience. We met almost nobody at our church, hustling in and out of Mass with our kids while I hunched in pain and avoided eye contact, but one of the exceptions was a friendly man who had seen me give the talk in New York where I almost wept. It turned out that he had moved his large family to a big house in the well-paved part of town because he had fallen ill with Lyme on his farm, in the horse country to the north, and lost years to waves of crippling exhaustion.

In the tiny nursery school where we placed our daughters, in a class with seven sets of parents, I overheard another father mention Lyme in passing during the welcome picnic. With a brazen rudeness that was entirely alien to my former self, I inserted myself into the conversation and grilled him about his experience.

"Yeah," he said, "I had a tick in me at the start of the summer—we did a little camping trip out by Pound Ridge, and I probably picked it up there. And I got something that looked kind of like the bull's-eye, and the doctor was going to give me antibiotics—but then my test came back negative, so he told me I was fine, no need to take them."

"And then . . . ?" I'd become a weird kind of glutton for other people's stories.

"Well, then I felt kind of fluey, you know, for a few weeks, kind of shitty . . . and then I woke up one morning and I literally couldn't move my hand. It was just curled into a fist, and my whole body was on fire." He shook his head, marveling at the memory.

"Did you go back to the doctor?"

"Nah, I knew enough to go to one of the specialists, this guy down in Bridgeport who treats people long-term—we know some other folks who've gone to him. He set me up with a strong course of doxycycline, with some other stuff too, some herbs and supplements. I'm still taking the doxy"— he rubbed his balding scalp—"and what they say about it making you sensitive to sun is true: I burned like crazy this summer. But it did the trick. It took a few months, but now I feel much better."

He went on talking, but my mind was fixed with hope and envy on the *I feel much better.* The guy was a little bit like me, or at least the *me* that I had imagined becoming after our big move—he was a stockbroker from the city who had moved his family out, bought the big house, settled into a more relaxed style of life, and every time I saw him he seemed personally happy in the way that I wanted to be: chill and casual at school functions, charmingly ironical in conversation, with plenty of time for his kids, their school, their country life. His wife was a doctor who, in their new, relaxed existence, had time to become a champion crocheter; her sweaters fetched top dollar at the school's silent auction. Lyme had hammered them, but they had snapped right back, so you *could* snap right back, so *we* could snap right back, and the happy Connecticut life would be waiting for us too . . .

But just in that same little school, there were other, less encouraging examples. One of the mothers had been stricken in her legs; she spent a year taking oral antibiotics with no result, and only IV treatment had finally burned the symptoms out of her thighs. She talked about it like a war veteran, hollow-eyed and traumatized. The school secretary had spent years ill, without a diagnosis. After further years of treatment, she still seemed foggy, dazed.

Other parents were marked in various ways by the sickness even if they hadn't fallen ill themselves. One mother who lived in a small house in one of the bigger nearby towns, in a neighborhood with postage-stamp backyards, brought her kids out to our spread for a playdate. She let them range across the lawns but spent the entire hour keeping strictly to our patio and stone walk, with occasional interludes atop a tree stump. It turned out that she and her husband had researched town-by-town tick prevalence when they made their own move from the city, and chose their neighborhood precisely for its lack of the rural picturesque.

"Those stone walls," she murmured with a pained gesture at one of our property's most attractive features, "they're just *heaven* for chipmunks. And you *do* know that mice and chipmunks carry as many ticks as actual deer."

We did not, but we were learning.

This secret-handshake, hidden-knowledge feeling extended into my professional life, which still called me into CNN greenrooms for a little while after we moved north. There as everywhere, I found myself babbling about my sickness, and there, too, I kept meeting people, usually semi-famous TV talking heads who lived in the New York or Long Island suburbs, who had their own wild stories. The political strategist with a brain-tumor diagnosis that turned out to be neurological Lyme. The prominent pundit whose left cheek still drooped slightly from Lyme-induced Bell's palsy. The Fox News host whose Lyme had been treated with antibiotics for a few months and who had lived with permanent back pain and insomnia ever since.

So our experience of returning to New England was like coming into one of those places in literature or film where the surface of beauty and neighborliness conceals a dark secret. Except, instead of the human sacrifice in *Midsommar* or the small-town stoning in "The Lottery," it was the widely shared understanding that the price of all those lovely lanes and stone walls was the possibility that you could lose years, or more, to Lyme.

And the disconnect between this understanding—shared

not by some isolated, marginalized, easily dismissed tribe, but by wealthy, educated types just a stone's throw from New York—and the official line from doctors was consistently startling. Even our new family doctor, the lovely, intelligent man who had suggested antibiotics and clearly believed that I had Lyme, did not believe that the chronic form of the disease was a big problem. His training taught him that it wasn't, and his private experience as well: He had been infected himself three times, and each time he recovered with a quick dose of antibiotics. So when Abby, fresh from an unexpected encounter with an exhibit of chronic-Lyme testimonials at the local library—including a photo shoot of gaunt, lost-looking patients, some of them surrounded by hundreds of prescription bottles—asked him if he thought it was safe to raise kids in this part of the country, he looked at her as if the question had never even occurred to him.

"I've just learned to tuck my pants into my socks when I mow the lawn," he told her reassuringly, like a man dismissing the most minor of annoyances. Which, for him, it was.

He also sent me to other doctors, Lyme-skeptical doctors, as a complement or counterpoint to the Maverick, of whose work he clearly disapproved. One of them was a Yale rheumatologist, with a honking WASP affect and a role in Lyme debates going back to the early years of the disease, who gave me a long lecture on my own misinterpretation of my symptoms. Maybe I had been infected once, he conceded, but after so much treatment, the disease simply had to be gone, and I was mistakenly linking my antibiotic experiences to gradual changes in my body that had nothing to do with any drugs.

This doctor diagnosed me with fibromyalgia and urged me to ditch antibiotics and try antidepressants again. When I explained that I simply couldn't go off antibiotics for even a week without returning to total incapacity, he suggested, like all the Washington doctors before him, that the incapacitation was mostly in my head.

So in a way there was a deep mystery here, of medicine and sociology combined, in which parallel worlds and narratives somehow coexisted in the same region, the same towns, even the same social circles—a medical divide much stranger than the political divides between Fox News and MSNBC viewers, say, or white evangelicals and white liberals, because of how completely the worlds of *Lyme is no big deal* and *Lyme is devastating* overlapped. (So completely, in fact, that I later learned that the wife and partner of my family doctor was the Maverick's own primary care physician.)

The deeper I went into the world of the chronically sick, the more people I met, the more testimonials and case histories I read, and the more I familiarized myself with the scientific background of the debate, the more impossible—and infuriating—it seemed that an entire medical establishment could be ignoring, denying, and dismissing the scale of suffering taking place all around them, not in some far-distant or exotic place but in their own hometown, their children's schools, the street or house next door.

But then again, I could also see how the divide sustained itself, because the deeper I went into the world of chronic sickness, the more I could feel the tug of paranoia, the sense that *the world is not as I had imagined and who knows what else might be true.* I could feel the experience of illness and bafflement remaking me, and I could see in other people how far this remaking could go—well beyond just taking extra antibiotics and doubting the wisdom of the CDC, into a more comprehensive rejection of any establishment wisdom, any mainstream consensus.

There was a questing spirit in many sufferers, an openness to experiments and personal experience and unlikely sources of wisdom. But there was also an inevitable conspiratorial side, such that the same person who knew the scientific literature chapter and verse might also start lecturing me on how the media was bought and paid for by Big Pharma or explaining that Lyme was probably a bioweapon. Listening to them, it was easy enough to put yourself in the shoes of doctors like Allen Steere and many others, getting their letters with an insane list of symptoms, listening to the attendant paranoias, and concluding that this must be *some kind of psychiatric illness*.

Then, too, there was the uncertainty and ambiguity in the testimonials that I found myself reading, in search of advice but also simple hope. For people who had become severely ill with Lyme, even the most optimistic narratives often ended the way Polly Murray's family story did—with incomplete recovery, or frequent relapses, or mysterious sequelae, or treatment that just went on and on.

Again and again, I would find a "Lyme blog" filled with optimistic early posts when the writer started treatment, and then click ahead to more recent posts and find that years later they were still struggling, still trying new therapies, often running low on hope and money both.

Combine this inability to recover with the variability of symptoms, the inevitable blurring of physical and mental suffering, and the difficulty determining when you actually fell sick, and you get the many Lyme accounts that seem written to *unpersuade* the skeptical—to give them more reasons to doubt the chronic cases and ratify their own confidence in simple rules, simple regimens, four-weeks-and-you're-done.

"I have never been comfortable in my own body," begins Porochista Khakpour in her 2018 Lyme disease memoir *Sick,* which is a powerful account of the mysteries of illness and embodiment—if you assume that chronic Lyme exists. Indeed, it makes sense that a chronic illness would be more likely to afflict someone whose flesh felt sensitive or vulnerable or compromised to begin with: After all, most people who get Lyme disease get better, so the people who don't, the people whose immune systems can't clear the infection without dramatic interventions, are presumably more likely to experience that vulnerability in other ways as well.

But if you don't accept the chronic theory, if you read a story that begins like Khakpour's with a skeptic's biases and assumptions, then her book's pervasive ambiguities, her uncertainty about where her illness ends and her natural self begins, would tend to confirm all of your skepticism about the disease and its alleged victims.

Likewise with less literary accounts. During my descent, the leading celebrity with chronic Lyme was Yolanda Hadid, a *Real Housewives of Beverly Hills* star, whose background and persona were calibrated to confirm the biases of anyone who believes that many chronic Lyme patients are attention seekers, self-dramatizers, menopausal women scripting more melodramatic versions of their own ordinary lives.

It was easy enough, against this backdrop, to imagine your way into the mindset of the typical Lyme-skeptical doctor in the greater Connecticut area. You see a lot of Lyme patients, you prescribe the standard regimen for most of them, and a lot of them get better. If *you* get Lyme disease, you probably get better, too, giving you a personal experience to set against all the wilder accounts in your community.

Your patients who don't get better, meanwhile, are likely to drop out of your practice when your treatments don't seem to help them. Instead of seeing them and following them across months and years of struggle, you lose track of them until they resurface via anecdote or brief encounters. And when they do, chances are that they're trying something weirder even than a lengthy course of antibiotics (that father who moved to town from horse country was in the medical supply business, and he eventually arranged to treat himself with hyperbaric oxygen therapy, flooding his bloodstream with oxygen inside a pressurized chamber, in the privacy of his own home) . . . or they've picked up extremely paranoid-sounding ideas about the medical system . . . or they claim to have discovered that they have some *other* chronic condition in addition to their Lyme disease . . . or they've adopted some fad diet . . . or they talk a lot about how "toxins" and other pollutants make people sick . . . or they've become vaccine skeptics . . . on and on and on, through a varying list that consistently gives you a reason to extend them sympathy but not belief.

Then, too, "you," the doctor in this narrative, are more likely to be a man (the gender imbalance in medicine is diminishing, but the profession still skews male) and "they," the patient, are more likely to be a woman. Men are somewhat more likely than women to be diagnosed with Lyme disease, but women are more likely to be diagnosed with the contested, chronic form. From the old "Lime disease" japes in medical journals down to the somewhat more circumspect present, this imbalance is another reason why so many doctors suspect that chronic Lyme isn't really Lyme, that it falls instead into a basket of mysterious "female problems" that have labels and symptoms, but no clear pathogenic cause.

An alternative possibility is that women are more likely to seek help for recurring problems and men are more likely to play the tough guy—like the Fox News host I mentioned, who described his constant pain and sleeplessness as stuff "I just live with," dismissing the medical carousel. But the fact of the gender breakdown, and the fact that women generally tend to be more interested in holistic medicines and mind-body connections and other places where the medical shades into the psychological and the spiritual (just as they are more likely to practice a religion), are further elements reinforcing the confidence of medical practitioners, male medical practitioners especially, that the weirdness of chronic Lyme disease can be dismissed as something difficult, even tragic, but nonetheless fundamentally unreal.

As THESE REALIZATIONS GREW ON ME THAT FALL AND WINTER, I became determined to be the exception to this pattern—the Lyme patient who didn't get tugged too far into the paranoid realm, the Lyme patient who experimented only with treatments that had some kind of clear basis in the material and quantifiable, the (male, conservative, *New York Times* columnist) Lyme patient whose account, once I was better, would be more convincing to skeptics influenced by sexism and wary of reality-television stars. Above all, I would be the exception to the pattern I kept seeing in all my reading, all my conversations: the Lyme patient who actually did get fully better, with no caveats or recurring complications, and who proved in my recovery both the reality and the treatability of the disease.

That was the idea, at least. But as days and weeks and months passed without recovery, it was inevitable that I, too, would begin to conduct my own experiments. Not the really crazy stuff, I told myself—not the sweat lodges and frequency machines and bee venom—but at least doses of the herbs that appeared so often in the Lyme literature, with names like cat's claw and artemisia and Japanese knotweed. These were things that I could buy online and take myself, take by the handful sometimes, in the hope that they would speed my recovery along. Soon my bedside table began to look like those photos in the library exhibit, those showcases of chronic desperation—the little pill bottles of antibiotics joined by others, a spreading, multiplying army from the Nature's Bounty aisle in the local pharmacy, that did not entirely inspire confidence that I was keeping my sanity intact.

And in spite of all the evidence around us of people in similar straits, all the photo exhibitions and advertisements for Lyme support groups, the possibility that I might be in the grip of a strange mental obsession was something that a person living with me could still occasionally believe. Under the Maverick's care, I finally had a positive blood test, but it was positive for *Bartonella,* one of the debated coinfections, not for Lyme. My Lyme tests continued to return two or three reactive antibody bands out of the officially necessary five: enough for the dissenters but well short of the CDC standard. Meanwhile, my descriptions of symptoms varied so much, the explanations of how the infection persisted sounded so baroque, my mood swings were so palpable and my desperation so intense as to make me seem the most unreliable of narrators where my own condition was concerned.

So part of my growing desperation in those days was a desperation for physical proof, some overt sign or symptom that would make it easier for people around me to see my illness as something objective and definitively real. The closest thing I had to offer was the flares of redness across my skin, like the one in the Boston hotel room, which I took to photographing, my own private exhibition. These, at least, were something visible, something I could show.

But now imagine yourself as my wife, locked in a rambling house with a new baby and two daughters under six, with a sleepless, pain-racked, disease-obsessed husband who occasionally comes downstairs, strips off his shirt, and demands that you examine the red streaks on his back. Yes, the strange local culture we had entered, with its countless chronic cases and pervasive tick anxiety, supplied some modest reassurance that I wasn't simply mad. But insanity and paranoia and raw panic can envelop regions and cultures as well as individuals, and there's no necessary reason that a single patient—like, say, your own husband—couldn't also be participating in some kind of mass delusion, the self-reinforcing madness of the crowd.

"Are you sure you didn't just make those with your rubbing?" she would ask, gently, carefully—not challenging me, exactly, but raising a question that hung over our house, our marriage, our every day and night.

IN THE MIDST OF THAT WINTER, SOMEONE ELSE ASKED IT more directly. It was now the most intense phase of the Republican primary, the peak of what turned out to be a futile anti-Trump resistance among the conservative intelligentsia, and I was channeling my pain into denunciations of his take-over, and the supine cowardice of the institutional GOP. After one particularly demagogic stretch, my reader's brain suddenly thought of the parallels between the Trump campaign and the candidacy of Greg Stillson, a populist politician in Stephen King's novel *The Dead Zone*. In that book, and in its film and TV adaptations, a psychic named Johnny Smith is given the preternatural revelation that Stillson will start a nuclear war, and decides, after much anguish, to attempt an assassination. His plot fails, but when Stillson is in peril, the demagogue picks up a little kid as a human shield—a move that destroys his candidacy and saves the world.

Without thinking much about what I was doing, I plucked a clip of the baby-hoisting moment from the movie version and posted it to Twitter, saying something like "Maybe this is how the Trump campaign will end." Two hours later I got a call from my editor, who told me that the internet was reacting as though I'd called for Trump's assassination. *Oh, come on,* I thought, but I took the tweet down and posted a mild apology. Then we went to the mall— myself, the girls, the baby, my wife.

We were eating Chick-fil-A when the call came:

Mr. Douthat, it's the Secret Service.

The Secret Service?

We need to speak with you.

Uh, sure. We're at the mall right now, I'm with my kids, how can I arrange . . .

We're waiting at your house.

And so they were, two agents plus a local policeman brought along in case they needed someone to keep an eye on me, just the thing to seal Abby's disastrous return to her hometown. They interviewed me at length, and I managed to convince them that the tweet had been a pop culture reference gone awry, that I had no intention of harming Trump or any other politician, that I was just a man who had made a blunder on the internet, like so many foolish journalists before me.

But they still had to search our basement and our attic, looking for munitions I might have stored or a bomb awaiting assembly, while I tried to explain to our five-year-old and three-year-old why the law had come for Daddy. Then, finally, they had to interview my wife—away from me, in case Abby needed to convey to them that she was actually a prisoner, that I was putting on a smooth front to conceal my maddened interior, that she and the children needed to escape.

Ma'am, do you have any worries about your husband's mental health?

God bless her, she said no.

But of course she did have exactly those worries, even if for her the relevant King novel wasn't *The Dead Zone* but *The Shining*—the family sealed away in a vast and haunted hotel, the wife tiptoeing around the unstable husband, humoring his moods, hoping his sanity holds, trying to protect her offspring and herself from the combination of paternal breakdown, snowbound isolation, and the ghosts.

I preferred the novel; she found Kubrick's adaptation scarier, with its emphasis on Jack Torrance's private demons over and above the supernatural. But either way, the analogy held. When people asked how we were doing, together in our Connecticut dream house as winter closed around us, that was the reference I would reach for.

"It's just like *The Shining*—except we're both writers."

.   .   .

BUT THIS, TOO, SUGGESTS A FINAL REASON WHY THE MEDI-
cal divide sustains itself: the sense among outsiders to the
controversy, even sympathetic ones, that the whole chronic-
Lyme story is a little too much like a dark fairy tale, a King-
grade horror story, to be accepted or believed. A vampiric
creature, lurking in the forest, that bites all but invisibly,
stealing your mind or body or your very life away. A mindless bacterium whose capacity for shape-shifting and survival
nonetheless suggests some malign intelligence at work. Family members falling ill like dominoes, as in Polly Murray's
story or Pamela Weintraub's book, like victims of a serial
killer in a slasher flick. An edifice of denial around the scale
of the infection, like villagers who propitiate some ruthless
beast while refusing to mention it to one another.

Journalists especially know that we are a storytelling spe-
cies, that we construct narratives around events that may not
actually belong in the same sequence, the same weave. So my
fellow journalists, even the most sympathetic ones, may very
naturally suspect that suffering people have latched on to the
chronic-Lyme explanation because it fits with the fairy-tale
narratives they remember from their childhood, the Jungian
archetypes lurking beneath the conscious, lucid mind.

The truth is that the experience of chronic illness does
change the way you relate to fairy tales, with their motifs of
metamorphosis and exile, witchy woods and hundred-year
enchantments. In seeking to give our girls a romantic childhood, we had wandered into the grimmest part of any fairy
story—the curse, the transformation, the imprisonment. So
even the banal Disney versions that played in our unhappy
home, keeping my daughters entertained while their parents
went through the motions of normality, could stir strong
emotions if I caught a piece of one at a particularly miser-

able moment. "When I'm human, as I hope to be," blared the soundtrack from *The Princess and the Frog,* its unhappily transmogrified creatures singing about their former, pre-enchantment selves: "When I'm myself again, I want just the life I had." Or the erstwhile prince in *Beauty and the Beast,* locked away inside his castle, waiting for the moment when his fur falls away and his claws become human hands again . . .

My subconscious, too, picked up on the dark-enchantment theme. In my fitful hours of sleep, I would often find myself in gothic dreams, usually with the same basic plot and setting. I was in a large building, a version of my own house, draped in semidarkness with a few lamps lit here and there. I wandered the halls and rooms and suddenly became aware that someone else was in here with me, some group of invaders—sometimes just housebreakers but more often something more fitted to the setting, chalk-faced vampires or gaping zombies, an intrusion of supernatural horror that I was helpless to resist.

Whenever I had these dreams, I would wake up to a surge of symptoms, usually a ruthless pulsing in my head. The vampires evaporated, the reality of invasion remained.

Which is the only thing that can be said, ultimately, to the skeptical, *it sounds too much like Stephen King* suspicion.

Sometimes, the darkest fairy tales are real.

4

The Country of Suffering

THE WINTER PASSED; MY PAIN AND DESPERATION DIDN'T. So when spring came—the spring of 2016, with Trump close to wrapping up the Republican nomination—that desperation drove me to abandon the pulsing regime and, with the Maverick's acceptance but clearly not his approval, try intravenous antibiotics instead.

The nearest doctor who administered IV antibiotics for Lyme was in a town across the New York line. I didn't want to put a stent into my arm—along with the risk of infection, it would keep me from even lifting my infant son—so I decided to drive the forty minutes to the clinic every single day, to sit in an armchair and let the new doctor and nurses fill me with Rocephin, at the not-covered-by-insurance cost of eight hundred dollars every week.

We were struggling to keep our bank balance level as it was, and so for the first time as an adult I had to ask my father for a gift of money. But there was no question in my mind that a month or so of IV was worth the gamble, worth the price. What was a few thousand extra dollars, set against the possibility of leaping quickly back to health? Frankly, if money alone could have guaranteed a swift recovery, I would have emptied every remaining dollar from our savings, taken out a second mortgage, and gone to my dad like the prodigal son asking for a full inheritance advance. In my straits, I felt like I had grasped a crucial secret: that good health is basically a superpower, which I had wasted once but never again, and any amount of money lost on treatment could be earned back, with interest, if only I had those superhuman powers back.

Where the Maverick was choleric and opinionated, the IV doctor was a saturnine character who wore Hawaiian shirts and dropped cryptic remarks and let me rant and rave about my symptoms without venturing strong opinions of his own. He certainly didn't try to cheer me up when I slumped in his chair and gave vent to my despair. "Feels like you just want to crawl into the woods and die, huh?" he would say cheerfully, checking the antibiotic drip.

Where the Maverick was an experimenter and a theorizer, mixing treatments and recalibrating prescriptions quickly if something didn't seem to work, the New York doctor was a grinder, willing to prescribe multiple drugs but mostly intent on using his IV drip to wear the sickness down. From the outset, he declined to make any predictions about how long I would need treatment. "We usually get people better," he would say, "but it takes how long it takes."

This strategy made the Grinder a particular target for the guardians of the medical consensus, who at one point hauled him before New York's medical review board, seeking to suspend his license. Out of all the treatments recommended by Lyme dissidents, IV antibiotics attract the most ire from the skeptics, and probably do the most to sustain the establishment's certainty that, whatever is going on with chronic-Lyme symptoms, the dissidents are dangerous and wrong.

There are some good reasons for this. All long-term antibiotic treatment carries health risks, but IV treatment is particularly likely to produce not only side effects but complications from the injection process. Patients have died from infected catheters and from the bacterium *C. difficile,* which can take root in the intestines when normal, healthy gut bacteria are killed off by antibiotics. Rocephin, the main IV drug, can cause various complications that need to be monitored with regular blood work (which the Grinder always ordered for me, I should note). To make a longer IV regimen the standard treatment, then, you would want definitive evidence of improvement, and so far, clear evidence has not been forthcoming. Absent such proof, the danger and expense of long-term treatment makes it look, to critics, like a way for physicians to milk patients of their money while exposing them to unnecessary risk.

That summer I became a potential exhibit for this argument. I started IV treatment in June, pinning my hopes not on any study but on individual testimonials—some from Lyme survivors I'd met, some gleaned from wee-hours scrolling through message boards—from people who had rapidly improved when they switched from oral to IV.

Quickly everything became worse. The Rocephin swept through me, causing reactions wherever I was symptomatic. If I had weakness or tingling in my legs, I drummed and stomped while I sat and took the drip. If I had pain in my chest, I found myself rubbing desperately at my pectoral muscles. If I had dizziness or aching in my head, it felt like a plume of fire blazed up my neck and through my skull.

Afterward I would guzzle water and sit slumped in the Grinder's waiting room. The other chairs were often occupied by wasted-looking young people accompanied by exhausted-looking parents, while the walls were plastered with thank-you notes from patients who had passed through this regimen and come out restored. Then I'd stagger around the nearby supermarket buying chocolate or hummus, and sit for a long time outside in the heat, dazed or crying, before attempting the drive back.

Often I would make the drive intentionally long, taking back roads, finding parks to wander in, churches in which to pray. One church had an outdoor calvary, a crucifixion scene on a hill above the church parking lot, with a flight of twelve steps leading to the wooden cross. I began stopping there to say prayers while kneeling on the first step of the dozen, and then the next day on the second step, telling myself that when I reached the top, the cross, I would have done enough IV treatment to begin to see some difference—or, better still, to actually feel well.

I had a decent day on step six, kneeling and praying half-way up. But the next five days were all worse, pain washing over me as I drove and knelt and prayed, the Rocephin lingering in my system and setting fires everywhere, a blaze without relief. On the twelfth day I didn't bother with the steps: I just went into the empty church and lay down for a while in the nave, halfway down the row of pews, my arms stretched toward the altar in supplication under the saints' and angels' stained-glass gaze.

So it went for weeks. On the roads or in our house, in the daylight or the dark, I would scrutinize my reactions to the Rocephin—as June became July and July August—in hopes of tracking some improvement, some diminishment of pain. Sometimes I would tell Abby that I thought it was working—which was true in the sense that it was clearly doing *something*. And I would tell her that I thought I might be getting better—which was, outside of one optimistic day in seven, a self-delusion or a lie.

She knew it, and I knew she knew it, which made that summer long and brutal, the worst days of our married life. Under the influence of whatever the Rocephin was doing, I finally felt the brain fog that so many Lyme patients talk about, descending like a cloud over my mind, and my capacity to write—the one thing that had been preserved for me throughout my illness—began to slip away. With the cloud came, for the first time in my life, a suicidal current in my thoughts—temporary like all my symptoms and therefore survivable, but still a repeated pulse of *just kill yourself, just kill yourself, just kill yourself* that lasted anywhere from a few minutes to an hour before it fled.

I had a book contract from before the illness, for a book about Pope Francis. In a fit of optimism—the IV would work, it *had* to work, because something had to work—I had planned a month's leave from my column that summer to work on it. I took the leave as planned, but I didn't use it for any sort of writing. Instead I left the house, telling Abby I was off to work, and then sat stupefied at local coffee shops, producing maybe a sentence on a good day, or else wandered the shady streets of the town, a ghost, an exile, a ruin. Sometimes I fell asleep on park benches—a scandalous sight, probably, in the immaculate town park. I went to movies—I was still writing film reviews, though I don't recommend relying on my takes from that summer—and fell asleep in them as well.

Back at home, both the land and the house seemed poisoned, corrupt. It turned out that there was an infestation of immense ground wasps, giant, buzzing cicada killers, that built mounds in August in the cracks between our flagstones and hung menacingly around our kids. The exterminator, a gaunt, poisoned-looking man, came out regularly and killed them, but he told us that he'd never seen so many, that even his treatments couldn't rid us of them all. Inside the house there were periodic plagues of insects: a carpet of ladybugs in the sunroom, a burst of wasps from the attic, and, crawling out of the walls, what we called the "slow flies," lazy, erratic black insects that hung around our kitchen and bathrooms. They were there waiting for me when I rose early to piss, hovering and buzzing while my legs vibrated or my chest burned, easy to swat but never gone for good.

In the evenings I went out to water the garden that we'd planted around our house, part of the attempt to playact normalcy in hopes that the acting would become real. I would stand with the hose spitting in the midst of the kind of New England summer evening that I had imagined all those years in Washington, D.C., now filled with hatred for the landscape around me, and thinking about how much I would give up for even an hour of ordinary feeling—the ordinary taste of a soda or beer, the ordinary satisfaction of collapsing exhausted onto a sofa, the ordinary feelings of stress or agitation or exasperation that seemed like such burdens in the life I had before.

Or I would lie on the flagstones, my spine pulsing, looking for airplanes high above, and beg God for some kind of help.

AROUND CHRISTMASTIME IN MY FIRST YEAR OF ILLNESS, THE popular pseudonymous online writer Scott Alexander wrote a short essay entitled "How Bad Are Things?" about his experience as a practicing psychiatrist seeing patients "in a wealthy, mostly-white college town consistently ranked one of the best places to live in the country." You would think, or at least hope, he wrote, that true misery would be rare among its fortunate inhabitants. But in fact, "every day I get to listen to people describe problems that would seem overwrought if they were in a novel, and made-up if they were in a think-piece on The Fragmentation Of American Society."

Some of these encounters represented the selection bias that comes with seeing the people most likely to end up visiting a psychiatrist—people suffering from mental illness, people with drug problems, people coping with a cascade of family tragedy. But Alexander argued that if you ran the statistics on chronic pain and personal trouble, he was actually getting a clearer version of how much misery exists even in the most privileged places in the world. The true scale of even upper-middle-class suffering, he suggested—encompassing everything from childhood or marital abuse to drug and alcohol addiction to all the different forms of chronic pain—was at once sweeping and invisible, at least to healthy people circulating among other healthy people.

In the same way that "we filter for people who are like us intellectually and politically," he wrote, "we also filter for misery," so that the suffering around us passes unheard and unseen.

To get sick and fail to get better is to realize the harsh truth of this insight. Human beings have a great capacity for kindness, empathy, and help, but we are more likely to rise to the occasion when it is clearly an *occasion*—a moment of crisis, a time-bound period of stress. In the aftermath of a hurricane, society doesn't usually fragment; it comes together in solidarity and support. Likewise with families and individuals facing suffering in the moment that it descends, or when a terrible arc finally bottoms out: Not always, but very often, people behave well, with great generosity, in the face of a mortal diagnosis, a mental collapse, an addict's nadir. Not least because in those circumstances there are things you can clearly do, from the prosaic—making frozen dinners for a suffering family—to the more dramatic and extreme, like flying across the country to help drag a friend into rehab.

But when the crisis simply continues without resolution, when the illness grinds on and on and on—well, then a curtain tends to fall, because there isn't an obvious way to integrate that kind of struggle into the realm of everyday life. It's not clear what the healthy person is supposed to *give* to a friend or family member who isn't dying, who doesn't have some need that you can fill with a discrete act of generosity, but who just has the same problems—terrible but also, let's be frank, a little boring—day after depressing day.

"Pain is always new to the sufferer, but loses its originality for those around him," the nineteenth-century French writer Alphonse Daudet wrote of his experience of a different spirochetal infection, syphilis, whose pain could be managed but in his case never cured. "Everyone will get used to it except me."

Or alternatively, in an age of scattered friendships and virtual connections, *everyone will forget about it except me*. That was how I experienced relationships as my initial descent gave way to the endless-seeming cycle of treatments and symptoms, of minor lifts and major falls. Having left our personal and professional circles behind in Washington, with my core group of college pals already scattered around the country and the world, I became accustomed to the surprised reactions of friends and relatives when we reconnected and they found out that I wasn't feeling better yet. After all, months had passed since we'd last spoken, and I clearly wasn't dying, so I must be better, I must be on the mend. Especially since they could encounter me every week or even daily on the internet, in my persona as a newspaper columnist and Twitterer, in which I performed normalcy, curating the self that I exposed, editing all the darkness out.

Oh, you're still *sick? I'm so sorry* . . .

So you're saying you're in pain every day? As in, you're in pain right now . . . ?

Well, your columns have been good . . .

Mixed in with the surprise, I always heard a hint of disbelief—but then, I was conditioned to hear it, and probably I was being unfair to their well-meaning incomprehension. Certainly I was being unfair in wanting something from them, some help or responsiveness or answer to my woes that I wouldn't have known how to offer had our positions been reversed. I hadn't known what to offer in my past experiences with friends who slipped into an abyss—in my twenties, for instance, when a friend with terrible depression would call me almost daily and then say nothing, or next to nothing, while I first babbled cheerfully and then lapsed into a useless silence of my own.

But maybe just my presence was more helpful than I gave it credit for at the time. In the first year of my illness, one of my college friends, a gregarious adventurer who lived and worked in South Korea, somehow made three separate visits to our unhappy house—once for a roommate reunion and then twice more randomly, making detours during his state-side business trips and appearing at our door. On one of these occasions he showed up with beer and pizza; on the other, rather more surprisingly, he appeared with his mother and his sister, who lived in Boston and somehow had been coaxed into some kind of caravan across New England.

In our friendship he had always been the enthusiast, the socializer, the omnivore; I had been his crotchety, complaining, *let's just go home early* wingman. Now those roles were accentuated into caricature. I basically fled when he showed up at our door with his tribe of relations, leaving Abby and the kids to welcome them, retreating into one of my various lairs to deal with the unbidden tears. When I finally crept downstairs and tried to act like a normal host, he stalked around the property cheerfully, bellowing like an ogre at our delighted girls and rattling off his mock-serious ideas for how we could improve our acreage: "Have you thought about putting a soccer pitch in your pasture, Ross? It'd be brilliant!"

It was a hardship, in a sense, to have him there; I certainly didn't take anything I recognized as enjoyment from these unexpected appearances. But when the shock of his sudden arrival faded, and especially once he gathered up his caravan and departed, I was almost pathetically grateful for the visit. His appearances were, in their way, acts of love and solidarity— offering no answer to my illness, no cure for our distress, save his solid physical presence, his good humor, and the proof, in all the miles he'd traveled, that he genuinely cared.

In a similar way, when I ranted profanely about my symptoms (*my fucking leg, this fucking pain in my fingertips, I can barely type*) or raged about the edifice of Lyme denial that I now saw everywhere I looked, I was grateful to the people who just listened, who broke into my monologuing with mild expressions of optimism and encouragement (*mild* was key; when people expressed strong optimism, it evoked a savage pessimism in response) but otherwise allowed me to express all my bottled-up and miserable and half-despairing thoughts, to lance the pulsing wound inside my psyche and let some poison out. Especially since every person who listened even occasionally was absorbing something that otherwise would have poured into the overflowing reservoirs of my closest family members, my parents and above all Abby.

Still, the fundamental reality remained what Daudet described. A friend could listen, another friend could visit, a family member could watch our kids or make us dinner, but there was a gulf fixed between my world and theirs, between my morning-to-evening experience of pain's variety and novelty and their inability to comprehend what it would mean to be sick every day, the same thing waiting every morning upon waking, without recourse or relief.

I could understand their bafflement, because I remembered what the term "chronic illness" had meant to me in the before times. Even with my mother's struggles as an example, I still associated it with the fatigue that comes after you've stayed up with a newborn baby, or the aches and pains you feel after exercising for the first time in months—suffering that was challenging but manageable, with recourse, in the worst case, to an exhausted sleep. Whereas the reality was pain that didn't let you relax, let alone sleep; pain that made your body feel like a cage around your consciousness; tension, always tension, the opposite of a Victorian lady picturesquely swooning on a couch. All this was an education, an experience of what it meant to be an embodied human being that could be endured but not really explained to someone whose body was still a home, a cooperator, a friend.

The only place to turn for real solidarity was the secret fraternity into which I had been initiated—not just Lyme patients, but the much larger group to whom a confession of chronic illness (and as I said, I confessed my situation to *everybody*) opened up. In my wanderings for work, in my visits to greenrooms and radio studios, in chance encounters and long online conversations, I constantly proved the truth of Scott Alexander's observation: There was extraordinary suffering everywhere, people dealing with pain of every variety, with conditions diagnosable and not, that had been largely invisible to me until I came into the country, cleared the filter, and experienced that misery myself.

I had made the journey in my thirties, earlier in life than many of my fellow countrymen. In general, the conversations I had were with men and women a little older than me, whose forties and fifties had taught them about all the things that can go wrong with a human body, all the places pain can enter and make itself at home. For the young, intense physical suffering was a lightning strike; for older people it gradually became the weather.

There was comfort there, of a sort: I was just living under a storm front that had rolled in a little early. But there was also a feeling of betrayal, because so little in my education had prepared me for this part of life—the part that was just endurance, just suffering, with all the normal compensations of embodiment withdrawn, a heavy ashfall blanketing the experience of food and drink and natural beauty. And precious little in the world where I still spent much of my increasingly strange life, the conjoined world of journalism and social media, seemed to offer any acknowledgment that life was actually *like this* for lots of people—meaning not just for the extraordinarily unlucky, the snakebit and lightning-struck, but all the people whose online and social selves were just performances, masks over some secret pain.

It's a commonplace observation by now that the internet transforms the experience of human social life into a meeting of facades, a whirl of bright, shiny images of happiness and health that conceal the real, embodied self. But chronic illness dramatically clarifies just how much this world of surfaces and curated selves lies to its inhabitants, to both the healthy and the sick. It lies to the healthy about the likelihood that they will one day suffer, the reality that even in a prosperous modernity the book of Ecclesiastes still applies. And it lies to the suffering, day after day, about how alone they really are.

To be sick and professionally online was an education in other people's hidden experiences. What I saw on my computer screen, the thrum of political argumentation punctuated by bursts of *happy news!, the engagement photo!!, the new baby!!!, the sunset scene from our vacation!!!, some really great exciting new job!!!,* was a version of what the unhappy teenager sees in the superficial online version of her high school's social life, what the divorced fifty-something with terrible back pain sees in a culture whose entertainments assume a world where everyone is forever twenty-five, what the grief-struck or addicted or depressed person sees in a world that has no capacity to integrate portraits of real suffering into its panoply of images.

My situation was different from these experiences, of course. Chronic Lyme reduces certain temptations that other forms of suffering heighten. I drank a moderate amount as a healthy person but not at all once I was sick, because alcohol made my symptoms worse to a degree that eclipsed whatever numbing effect it might have had. I tried painkillers of various kinds and quickly gave them up, because even when they reduced the burning and aching, they left untouched the deeper feeling of wrongness, of something alien beneath my skin, of a tension in my frame that nothing could relax. So neither opioids nor alcohol, the substances implicated in so much early-twenty-first-century American carnage, had much pull on me.

But raw despair, suicidal ideation, glimpses of the abyss— all that was there, worsened in a certain way because of the knowledge that neither a stiff drink nor a dose of OxyContin could do much about it, that even if I wanted to I couldn't numb myself, that the only solution was the most extreme and absolute and final.

I don't want to exaggerate the temptation that I felt, though, because I also always knew, as people suffering under the weight of true depression may not, that the worst of these feelings would pass not in weeks or months but in hours, once the symptoms abated in my skull and moved, say, to my stomach or my feet. This is the other distinctive aspect of Lyme, relative to other chronic conditions: Its masquerading quality means that you get to know what it feels like to have a lot of different kinds of illnesses, without ever knowing what it feels like to have a single condition permanently. So just as I can tell you what *brief* suicidal ideation feels like, I can tell you what it feels like to *temporarily* have symptoms associated with multiple sclerosis or Crohn's disease, chronic migraines or painful ulcers, syphilis or arthritis or peripheral neuropathy. But of course this is radically different from the experience of actually having one of those conditions every day and hour.

This difference means I have no way of knowing which is worse. But I can say, at least, that the switching, the predictable unpredictability, is its own special kind of torture. Indeed, I often told the friends who listened to my rageful blurts and angry monologues that I wished I just had a leg that didn't work, or an eye that couldn't see, or some other permanent incapacity that was at least the same day after day. This was an idiotic desire, because with my own illness there was clear and reasonable hope that I could actually get better, even if it took years instead of the months I had initially expected. But the idiocy of trading a lifetime's use of a leg for a faster reprieve from everything else tells you how bad that *everything else* felt, how crippling a constantly shifting wave of temporary symptoms can seem.

In 2014, three researchers conducted a survey of thousands of people diagnosed with Lyme disease whose symptoms persisted past six months, well into chronic territory, and compared their quality-of-life reports with those of people who had other serious conditions—diabetes and multiple sclerosis, the aftermath of stroke and heart attack, depression and PTSD. The survey asked the Lyme patients to estimate how many days out of thirty they felt beset in different ways—"days of bad sleep," "days limited by pain," "anxious days," and so on. Their average for each symptom category was between fifteen and twenty days of suffering a month; the average for "healthy days with vitality" was four days out of thirty. In terms of overall reported suffering, the chronic Lyme patients were above every other category of persistent pain; the only comparable condition was congestive heart failure.

I want to stress that I have no way of knowing what congestive heart failure feels like, and there are ways—more apparent to me now—in which, even at my worst, I was luckier than many other chronic Lyme patients. But we can table the question of relative suffering entirely and still say this much about tick-borne illness: As a primer on the sheer variety of physical pain, the diversity of ways and places that a human body can go wrong, it has few competitors.

THE IDEA OF ILLNESS AS AN EDUCATION, OF COURSE, IMplies that there is something *purposive* to the experience— taking us back to the landscape of the fairy tale, or upward to the idea of a providential God. And here I exaggerated when I said that little in my life had prepared me for my descent into chronic pain, because I definitely had a more religious upbringing—more intense and immersive, not just with more hours in the pew—than most people in my social class or professional peer group. And because I retained faith as an adult, I had that belief as a support structure, a bulwark against despair.

That said, my faith was also a pretty abstract and intellectualized thing. I had watched other people have mystical experiences as a kid, but I had always been more or less impervious to whatever currents were washing through the adults around me. I observed people—my parents, their friends, random strangers—being overcome with raptures with a cool sort of distance, believing that they were experiencing something real, something that merely psychological theories were inadequate to capture, and envying them that experience without feeling even a hint of anything battering at my defenses, any dove descending on my soul. I found the arguments for belief reasonable, the narrative of the Gospels compelling, the doctrines of Christianity attractive, but when I was asked, in the testimony-obsessed Pentecostalist churches we attended for a while, to *testify to how the Lord Jesus had come into your heart,* I had precious little to say for myself. Indeed, I found our ultimate destination, the Catholic Church, which we joined when I was a teenager, comforting in its absence of such questions, its emphasis on the reliability of the sacraments whatever your inward response, on the corporate rather than purely individual nature of salvation.

So the faith that I carried into chronic illness was, in a sense, the sort of faith that you might expect to bend or even break under the pressure of real suffering, the contrast between the brute reality of pain and my somewhat attenuated idea of God. Especially since the nature of the illness, the perpetual press of symptoms, meant that my always half-hearted approach to prayer collapsed completely. The idea of recollecting yourself, of quieting your mind, of seeking a stillness and a silence in which the divine peace might enter in—it all seemed impossible and absurd. The only kind of prayer I could manage was a desperate begging, a hopeless pleading in cool churches and the summer heat, a demand for help repeated endlessly without an answer.

One of the curiosities of the modern era is the way that the debate about whether a good God would allow human suffering, the eternal question of theodicy, has become a persuasive argument for atheism (or at least against Christianity) at the same time that actual physical suffering has in many ways declined. The world of mass infant mortality, rampaging disease, and endless toothaches had more faith in God's ultimate beneficence than the world of increasing life expectancy and effective pain management techniques.

Before sickness took me, I tended to assume this was because in a world with less everyday pain, the experience of suffering felt more outrageous, more unjust, than it did in a world where pain was too ubiquitous to be concealed or filtered out of everyday experience. And I still think there's something to this idea, since entering a permanent-seeming sickness did seem like an impossible outrage to my modern self at first—like some sort of ridiculous bureaucratic mistake.

But what I learned from my illness is that chronic suffering can make belief in a providential God, if you have such a thing going in, feel essential to your survival, no matter how much you may doubt God's goodness when the pain is at its worst. To believe that your suffering is *for* something, that you are being *asked* to bear up under it, that you are being in some sense supervised and tested and possibly chastised in a way that's ultimately for your good, if you can only make it through the schooling—all this is tremendously helpful to maintaining simple sanity and basic hope. *If God brought you to it, He can bring you through it,* read an aphorism in one of the doctors' offices I frequented: a neat distillation of what I wanted—and, more important, needed—to believe, in order to get up every morning and just try to hold my world together for another shattered-seeming day.

"A crutch for weak-minded people"—that's how the noted philosopher Jesse "the Body" Ventura once described religion. My pre-illness self would have disputed that description, but my sickened self would merely give it a tweak. *Absolutely* religion is a crutch, and it's not only useful for the weak of mind but for anyone dealing with severe weakness. You had better believe that I leaned on my belief in a silent, invisible God more in those miserable months, that miserable summer, than on any hope or notion or idea in any prior portion of my life.

Which is not to say the hope that my suffering had a purpose was entirely comforting when it came to the central thing I wanted—to get better, to be myself again, to shake free of the spell. Because if suffering is interpreted as a refining fire, then there's no guarantee, short of sainthood, that it will swiftly be withdrawn. (And if you examine the lives of the saints, not even or especially then.) In this sense, the real Christian answer to the "problem" of suffering is that we have the problem all wrong—that it's actually more mysterious when good things happen to good people than when bad things do, because if God gave His son to the cross, then a version of the same test is what every Christian should expect.

And if you conspicuously *aren't* virtuous—if you're mediocre at best and maybe even a little smug—and you get a dose of suffering, and you tell yourself that *maybe this will help me grow in virtue* . . . well, maybe it will, but then your reward for that growth might not be recovery and health. It might just be another spoonful of the same bitter medicine, or an even stiffer dose.

Such, at least, was my interpretation of the theology of suffering in those days. I feared what it implied, as I feared the God who had allowed this, and what He might consider allowing next.

This meant, in turn, that I also often despised the kindlier forms of providentialism, the talk of God's loving plan and whatnot, to which my savage mind replied, *Great, and what if His plan is for me to lose everything—not just health but money, not just money but my marriage and family? I wouldn't put it past Him at this point.*

But I was also looking for a happier narrative arc. I didn't want someone else explaining my suffering to me, any more than I would imagine someone enduring the sharpest grief—the death of a child, the sight of a loved one's body on a slab—would want me weaving their suffering into some pat and sunny story. At the same time, I wasn't at all content with the invocation of mystery that late-modern Christians are taught to offer when the problem of suffering comes up—the idea that it's all just a big unfathomability and all we can do is join our griefs together and lament. For myself I definitely wanted narrative, a sense of the arc of my life in the light of this disaster, the purposes of its Author in imposing this particular plot twist.

When I tried to educate my kids into religious belief, I sometimes told them to think of themselves as living inside a story, with God as the novelist and themselves as characters, inventions of a storyteller who had somehow entered into His own pages and given His creations freedom. ("In eternity this world will be Troy, I believe," muses a character in Marilynne Robinson's *Gilead,* "and all that has passed here will be the epic of the universe, the ballad they sing in the streets.") This Christian idea has secular variations: Even people who officially believe that the universe is purposeless and human existence is just one damn thing after another will find themselves enfolding their own experiences of suffering into a larger vision of the pattern of their life, looking for ways that great good came from great evil, discerning a warp and woof even if they find the idea of a weaver impossible to credit.

In my own case, I sometimes felt like the weave was almost visible. There was such a pileup of coincidence and strange repetition—the sickness arriving exactly with our son's conception, the echoes of Abby's childhood in our unhappy return to her hometown, my own hubris meeting its tiny crawling nemesis. But what kind of story was it? Were we trying to break out of some intergenerational repetition—having a third child after our parents in both cases stopped at two, having a son when my wife's family was all daughters going back two generations? Were we being chastised for our nostalgia, our attempt to chase a different version of our childhoods? Was this just a temporary fire we needed to pass through? Or was it a sign that we needed to entirely change our lives?

Trying to discern the answer was like staring through mottled glass at almost recognizable shapes. There was something there, I was almost certain of it, but I needed some different set of eyes to see what it meant, what was really happening in our story, and what the God who had sentenced us to purgatory expected from us now.

No clarifying vision was delivered, and at the end of that August I took a break from the Grinder's IV, loaded myself up with oral antibiotics, and drove in a stupor with Abby and the kids to Maine, to the mid-coast region where my mother had grown up and my relatives still lived. It was beautiful and awful: Those small towns and coves and islands were the landscape of so much remembered childhood happiness, and to be there again in this state was somehow more intolerable than anything. I walked the beaches of my youth in a daze, as thin again as I had been at seventeen. I watched the sunrise through eye sockets that burned; I heard the seagulls through ears that were always under pressure, as though I were fathoms deep beneath the sea. My children played on the sandbar, my infant son splashed in the saltwater puddles, and my beloved wife watched me watching them. A veil of pain was drawn between me and everything I loved.

On the last morning, I was up early as always and I carried my son, now six months old and heavy, down the long, low-tide strip of sand. The pain was mostly in one shoulder, though I knew it would be somewhere else soon enough. There was a spot where the sand gave way to barnacled rocks bewigged with seaweed, where the tide met the stones; sometimes in her youth, my mother had found sand dollars there. I had never found one in decades of looking, and over time it had become a game I played—*If I find one today, it means that God exists. If I find one today, it means that the girl I have a crush on has a crush on me. If I find one today, it means I'll get into the college I want. If I find one today, it means . . .*

Inevitably, I had been playing the game all that vacation week, casually glancing in the shallows as I waded with my kids.

If I find one it means I will get better.
If I find one it means I will get better.
If I find one it means I will get better.

On that last day, though, I was in too much pain to play. I held my son in my right arm, watching the seagulls sweep above, feeling the fire spread down my left arm and side. At a certain point, the combination of beauty and agony broke me, and I began to sob there, on the empty sandbar beside the flat, blue bay, while my son cooed curiously, and from somewhere in the depths I came out with a desperate, rasping croak.

"Help me, God. Why won't You help me?"

My eyes dropped to the water. There between my feet, as tiny as a nickel and as pale as a wedding dress, was the only sand dollar I have ever found.

5

An N of 1

WE CAME BACK FROM MAINE, BACK TO THE AUTUMN of the 2016 presidential election. The apples I'd imagined picking were falling to rot across our lawn, giving off the smell of vinegar when we stepped on them. By now the parts of the property closest to the house had been substantially refurbished: the garden planted where we'd torn the hedges out, the curtain drain dug, a generator installed to protect us from the winter's power outages, fences thrown up to keep our kids away from the lower pasture, and the whole outside painted a stark New England white.

Some of this had been done by my father, who took up the puttering-around-the-property role that I'd imagined myself playing. Some of it was the work of Luis and his team. And some of the work I did myself, though in hindsight I'm not sure how I dug the pit for the generator. The memory of shoveling it out in a sodden late-spring drizzle—six feet down, and then a long trench to the house, where the gas line connected—belongs to someone else.

But as we entered our second autumn in our dream house, the impossibility of the whole task became apparent.

The barn we hadn't touched, the pool we hadn't opened, the rotting fencing around the pasture, the dead trees poised to fall, the guest cottage where our tenant lived with a tree branch snaking its way into her foyer, the field overgrown and turning into marsh—it was all too much to be mastered by a man in my physical condition, a couple in our plight. If I wasn't going to get better (not a possibility I accepted, but one Abby had no choice but to consider), or if I was destined to spend years returning to myself (something I increasingly allowed), then this house was not a place where we could stay.

So we embraced the absurd humiliation of bringing back the local realtors and telling them that in fact the country life was not for us, and it was time to flip the house to someone else with deeper pockets and greater capabilities. Which, they assured us, we could do, and recover at least some of the money we'd sunk into it, because *it's such a lovely property, especially if someone from the city's looking for a second home,* and surely someone would love it as much as we did.

Meanwhile, since we definitely needed our family's help and we'd priced ourselves out of D.C. with our financial hemorrhage, we started looking at places in Connecticut that resembled the D.C. world that we'd abandoned—walkable urbanism, proximity to trains and restaurants and people, neighborhoods that would reduce the punishing, except-for-family isolation to which my illness had consigned my wife. And it quickly became clear that the most likely place for us was my own former hometown of New Haven, yet another weird circling back that seemed to fit somehow with whatever strange story we were inhabiting, even if I had no idea where its author intended us to finish up.

. . .

JUST BEFORE WE REACHED THE DECISION TO SELL, THERE WAS finally a real change in my condition. One of the oral antibiotics I'd brought with me to Maine was called Tindamax, a somewhat obscure drug that I had encountered in my obsessive readings of the online Lyme conversation. A Lyme doctor who kept his own blog cited it as one of his more successful prescriptions for chronic patients—mostly, he hypothesized, for its supposed penetrative power, the way it reached deep into infected tissue.

For a few weeks I took it without any noticeable result. But one day I happened to take the Tindamax in a sequence with another antibiotic—the Tindamax first, and then about thirty minutes later a couple of the amoxicillins I had lying around from the Reassurer's old prescriptions—and something unexpected happened. As the amoxicillin capsule dissolved into my bloodstream, the usual discomfort gave way to something stronger: I suddenly flailed and rubbed and gagged and tore off my shirt and scratched like a man turning wolf under a full moon. It felt like a full-body Herxheimer, as strong a reaction as any of my foot-drumming, head-burning experiences in the IV chair. It lasted about twenty minutes and then passed and left me spent.

Spent, but with the beginning of a crucial, treatment-changing insight. There were things I could take—the Tindamax to begin with, but then other things as well—that seemed to *expose* the bacteria somehow, to either force the cysts to change their shape ("cyst-busting," in the Lyme parlance) or else just coax the hidden corkscrews from their hiding places in my tissue, making them temporarily vulnerable to a blast of conventional antibiotics. On their own, the drugs I had been taking were like pickaxes chipping at a fortress wall or thimbles draining a great lake. In combination with Tindamax—or grapefruit seed extract or oregano oil or serrapeptase, and so on down a list of compounds that I began to use in the same sort of sequence—they felt more like tiny cannons or small buckets: still insufficient for a quick victory, but a real weapon in the fight at last.

Suddenly, for the first time in all my treatment, the physical reactions became predictable. If I took enough of these substances, I would feel worse in the old dissociated ways, with interior vibrations and dizziness and sporadic bursts of pain. If I then took an antibiotic, I would get a Herxheimer, guaranteed—a feeling that I was purging something as I scratched or rubbed or just moved the affected limbs or joints or muscles. Neither experience could be described, exactly, as feeling *better*, but after the Herxheimer there was usually a touch of physical relief woven into the exhaustion, and with both there was something I had desperately needed: a hint of actual control.

The idea that you need to make yourself feel worse in order to feel better is central to chronic-Lyme treatment. (And to other treatments, like chemotherapy, as well.) But it's also a point often fretted over by skeptics, who note that it can be a license for doctors to push their patients deeper into misery, with the promise that because a treatment makes you feel sicker it must be working, that it must just be the Herxheimer kicking in. It's a reasonable worry. Without a way to know for sure how far to go, or when to turn back, *the worse, the better* can be a dangerous philosophy.

I would like to say that I kept this in mind when I began

dosing myself with these combinations: that I listened to my doctors, who always urged caution, and heeded my anxious wife, who worried about me pouring drugs and herbs like so much gasoline into my burning body. But no, I had waited so long for a breakthrough, and I was reckless with my discovery. So over the course of a few September weeks, I simply doused myself with anything that seemed to have this "cyst-busting" effect, letting the experiment run 24-7, trying to make myself feel as terrible as possible—and the large doses did quickly make me feel terrible, bringing back frightening feelings of bodily weakness and tingling extremities and even the old terrifying chest pressure. I went back to the Grinder and his IV, and without telling him I would take handfuls of these herbs and supplements in advance of the appointments, making myself a spaced-out danger on the road, in hopes of exposing absolutely everything to the Rocephin's killing blast. And I would run the same experiments at home, while doing errands, at the car dealership, at the supermarket, waiting outside our children's school.

This led to some odd scenes. I remember jogging down the service road behind the dealership, literally tearing my shirt open and grunting because the action was happening somewhere deep inside my throat. Or coming back from a trip to get Chinese takeout, trying to contain myself in the restaurant and the car, and then flinging myself out as soon as I pulled into the driveway to run a lap, punctuated by Rockette-style leg kicks, around our upper lawn.

One night Abby was gone, the baby with her, to visit a friend—a rare escape for her, and a rare night alone with the girls for me. After putting them to bed I went to work, like Jekyll in his laboratory, bringing Hyde to life over and over again. A dose of herbs, another, another, more symptoms and yet more—and then finally the antibiotic, the Herxheimer, the stomping and thrashing—and then again, *again,* the same cycle long past midnight, wandering the house like it was the Gothic mansion in my dreams. All the while I imagined that the next blast would somehow take out everything lurking in my system, would drain the lake or bring the wall finally crashing down.

At a certain point in this reckless period, I had a conversation with a doctor at the University of New Haven, an academic researcher who studied all the various unexpected things that kill the Lyme bacteria (the sugar substitute stevia, for instance) after she recovered from her own long spell with the disease. I told her what I was doing, and she called it "chasing the Herxheimer," as if it were a common practice instead of the craziest experience in the world. She said she had spent months trying that herself, before realizing that a slow-and-steady pace was better. You simply couldn't kill all the bacteria with drugs anyway. "I douse it with bleach in a test tube and it recovers," she told me. The only way to recover your health was to reach a point where your immune system could bounce back and decisively suppress it.

So I became less extreme and just tried to work with my combinations a little more patiently and carefully, Herxheimer after Herxheimer, spacing them out every few hours instead of keeping up a constant pace. But in the extremity of my experimentation I had learned something decisive. Given a stockpile of antibiotics, the array of over-the-counter medications available on Amazon, and crowdsourced data from hundreds and thousands of Lyme sufferers sharing their experiences online, I could effectively become my own doctor, mixing and matching to gauge my body's reaction to different combinations, like a Lyme researcher working on a study with a sample size, an "N," of only 1.

These experiments quickly confirmed two realities for me, which I suspect apply to many Lyme patients struggling to recover. First, timing is everything. Because the bacteria can be easily attacked only when they're active in your bloodstream, taking two antibiotics in the morning or even dosing yourself through an IV in the afternoon is meaningless, or at best ineffective, if you aren't heavily symptomatic when you take the drugs. The key is to strike exactly when the symptoms strike, to take the drugs and the cyst-busting supplements when your shoulder starts to hurt or your mind fogs up or your leg flames or your bowels liquefy . . . because that's the time when there's something there to kill. Whereas to just follow the instructions on the prescription bottle is to waste your weaponry, like dropping bombs on Iwo Jima while the Japanese are dug in, too far underground for them to reach.

The second lesson of my self-doctoring is that even the aggressive protocols of Lyme doctors may understate how *many* Lyme-killing drugs you need to take to push the disease back, to reclaim a little space and sanity and life, to give your immune system what it needs to revive and join the fight.

"Like trying to put out a forest fire with a watering can" was how one Lyme patient described his experience with antibiotics, and the image fits with mine as well. To gain ground that fall and winter—and I did gain ground, at an impossibly slow pace but one still recognizable, compared with the nightmare months, as progress—I worked with the Maverick on a new three-drug protocol, tetracycline and rifampin and Bactrim, which I paired with the Tindamax and with the widening array of cyst busters recommended by the internet. That meant I was taking about twelve antibiotic pills a day, a physically safer dose than the IV course, but a far higher one as well.

But I went beyond even that. Without the Maverick's permission or knowledge—he was an extremely careful experimenter, demanding blood work to monitor every new prescription—I kept supplementing my course with antibiotics left over from the earlier doctors' prescriptions. Eventually those ran out and I began to supplement instead with antibiotics that I bought first from overseas pharmacies and then, for a while, from online pet stores—the same pills as the pharmacy, with weaker quality control but no need for a prescription, and fish or peacocks on the bottles. I remembered the version of myself that had been afraid to take the amoxicillin two years earlier, afraid of unknown side effects. Now I was the kind of heedless experimenter that doctors despair over, and that pharmaceutical regulations exist to protect and deter.

Meanwhile, with my doctor's knowledge, but without his approval for the scale of what I was doing, I also added in every non-prescription antimicrobial substance that any study, however obscure, suggested might kill Lyme bacteria in a test tube: cat's claw, stevia, goldenseal, andrographis—a whole range of things drawn from different herbalists, different laboratory work.

"If you take so many things, you won't be able to tell what works," the Maverick warned as he tapped away on the computer where he recorded symptoms, drugs, improvements. I knew I had become a frustrating patient—unable to follow his pulsing regime, disobedient and reckless in the things I tried—and that the advice he was giving me was entirely sensible. But in my case it still felt entirely wrong. My symptoms were so strong and so pervasive, the infection so aggressive and widely disseminated, that the reactions to everything I tried were also swift. I could tell within an hour of taking something whether it was touching the infected areas, because if it did I would quickly get a version of the itching, rubbing, flailing feeling in the symptomatic region. Likewise with the various things I tried as cyst busters—they would make me more symptomatic somewhere quickly, or else I would discard them, confident that they didn't work.

This confidence was the gift of that second fall and winter in Connecticut. I was not better in the sense of having fewer symptoms, certainly not healed in the way that I had spent the first year of my sickness hoping to achieve. No, I was very much a sick person, maybe not forever but clearly for some long span to come. But just as Abby took some encouragement from her own tasks that autumn—readying the house for sale in the spring and promoting her newly published book, which took her out of our shared nightmare and back into the normal world, to interviews and bookstore readings and other places where flies weren't crawling from the walls—so I took hope from the sense that I was gaining information, knowledge, with every drug course and herbal experiment, learning something new whenever something worked and even when it didn't.

My body was still occupied territory; my sickness still held sway. But I was beginning to understand and even anticipate my enemy, and for a time, small victories were enough.

. . .

In Susan Sontag's "Illness as Metaphor," an essay that every writer considering their own sickness is obliged to reckon with, the kinds of metaphors I've been using in this chapter—disease fighting as military combat, medicine as war—came in for withering treatment. They are part of "a simplistic view of the world that can turn paranoid," Sontag wrote from her seventies-era vantage point. "The fight against cancer has sounded like a colonial war—with similarly vast appropriations of government money—and in a decade when colonial wars haven't gone too well, this militarized rhetoric seems to be backfiring." Any so-called war on a serious illness, she suggested, was likely to resemble the conflict in Vietnam, with similar official optimism contrasting with pessimism among specialists and reporters, similar indifference to collateral damage ("it is thought that nearly any damage to the body is justified if it saves the patient's life"), a similar mythology of brutality ("unpleasant side effects of treatment are advertised, indeed overadvertised") somehow paving the road to victory.

Forty years later, a version of Sontag's heresy has become an orthodoxy among many critics of official medicine, and many mainstream medical practitioners as well. The holistic alternatives to the medical establishment, in particular, go out of their way to emphasize the image of *balance* instead of conflict, to stress that they're working with your body rather than launching a campaign on its territory, to insist that they're there to help the village save itself rather than razing it for the sake of illusory gains. Meanwhile, the psychological professions worry that martial metaphors imply a kind of Napoleonic agency-in-combat that sufferers don't really have, and risk passing a kind of judgment on the patient's capacities— *he lost his battle, she lost her fight*—that's cruel and unfair.

All of this seems sensible and compassionate. And yet, in going beyond the boundaries of official medicine, in discovering complex treatments that worked where simple ones had failed, I still found myself returning to military metaphors, indeed finding them inescapable every time I—*here I go again*—threw different drugs and herbs and compounds into the fray.

The bare facts demanded them. To have a chronic infection is to have organisms in your body that have disabled the defensive systems that normally exist to eradicate or suppress them. Your infected body *is* a terrain of combat, in other words, and a great battle has already been lost—or else, if the infection is simply eluding the defenses, your forces are scattered and unequal to the task. So you have to find reinforcements to send into the terrain that will kill the organisms that now own it, or attack in ways that are outside your current forces' capabilities. And when those invading organisms use their own defense mechanisms to evade your reinforcements, you need to discover and craft strategies (the right combination of medications, the right timing of the dose) that will overcome their defenses or flush them out of their redoubts.

Every time you take something that promises to kill off some of the bacteria, you effectively attempt a sortie, an attack—and there is a literal battle within your veins, your tissues, in which organisms either live or die. (Yes, the battle's actual participants are mindless, but so are bullets, bombs, mines, drones.) Then, over time, the symptoms either advance, filling entire limbs and swaths of muscle, the entirety of your digestive tract, the whole of your head, or else they retreat into small pockets of discomfort in joints and tendons, your temples or your eyebrows or your balls. And whether they advance or retreat all depends on which weapons you choose, how much fire you direct into your own system, and whether your strategies succeed.

Throughout, then, the idea that you are fighting for your health, your very life, doesn't feel like a misleading metaphor, because it doesn't feel like a metaphor at all. It's just the reality of trying to destroy a chronic illness, an invader, that has to die in order for you to live.

The strategic element in this reality is also very different from the assumptions many people make about experiments in treating chronic illness—that if you are treating yourself outside the bounds of the official medical consensus, you must be rejecting "Western medicine" in favor of the unempirical, searching out some mystical mind-body interface, embracing unfalsifiable theories of "energy" drawn from acupuncture or homeopathy.

This assumption flows naturally from the phenomenon I noted earlier, the confusing, highly personal way in which chronic sufferers talk about their symptoms. (If someone's suffering is diffuse and weird and ever changing, it's natural to assume that the path to improvement must be even more mysterious.) It flows from the way that a lot of people who haven't gotten fully better but have found a way to coexist with their disease, and function somewhat normally in the world, tend to testify or write about that coexistence—its ebbs and flows, its strange currents, the way it can be influenced for better or worse by psychological and spiritual realities. And it flows, I suspect, from the way sex stereotypes shape our thinking about chronic illness—because the fact that women are more likely to be diagnosed with chronic illness leads some people to assume that there's a particularly feminine psychosomatic element at play, and others to lapse into a kind of earth-mother mysterianism when they talk about recovery.

There is, obviously, real mystery here—an obvious interface between chronic illness and the outré, the outlandish, the bizarre. (You can flip ahead two chapters and read about the weirder stuff.) But there is also a lot of practical work before you push up against the mystery, and the initial task of battling my disease with half-understood medicines, the self-doctoring that I found myself doing, was in its own way intensely empirical and materially grounded—the most empirical work, in fact, that I have ever attempted in my life.

Empirical, to be clear, doesn't mean *meeting the rigorous standard for FDA approval.* But neither does it mean wandering a natural-foods store with a dowsing rod and popping whatever supplement the metal points you toward, or keeping a dream journal and then parsing it for subconscious codes that spell out the herbal remedies you need. Nobody who experiments on medicine's frontiers has to sally forth at random. They can follow the wisdom of crowdsourcing, the accumulated testimony of other sufferers, attacking their own N of 1 with the benefit of a larger sample, which, even if its results aren't subject to placebo-controlled trials or peer review, still offers *evidence* rather than pure guesswork, *data* rather than just individual anecdote.

A data set can be meaningful and useful and suggestive, in other words, even if it falls short of the standards that are set by official medicine in its bureaucratized, safety-first contemporary form. Nearly fifty years into the Lyme experience, with thousands upon thousands of sufferers and decades of experiments, such a data set emphatically exists—and it exists, above all, on the internet, which was a source of misery during my first year of sickness (all those happy facades on social media!) but, from then on, a source of help.

That help took the form of lists and conversation and testimony on Lyme message boards. It took the form of case histories enlisted in the debates between the various Lyme-treatment camps. It took the form of actual doctors' ruminations and reports: that Lyme doctor blogger who touted Tindamax, or another one in the Pacific Northwest who published all his different protocols with dosage information and suggestions for each coinfection. And it took the form of preliminary, not fully dispositive research, like that University of New Haven doctor's work on stevia—which, yes, I definitely took. Indeed, for almost everything that helped me, I found there was usually some physiological explanation for its effectiveness—maybe an explanation offered by a single experiment, a lone scientist's work, a specific doctor's hypothesis, but an explanation all the same.

Meanwhile, as the crowdsourced treatments that I tried were tested against reactions in my body, those tests also revealed internal patterns that had been invisible when I was at my most confused and helpless—consistent differences and similarities between different treatments, consistent changes in my symptomology when I got a cold or a stomach flu or seasonal allergies, consistencies in which part of my body reacted to which drug.

One of the most striking patterns involved the coinfection that I carried. When I first tested positive for *Bartonella,* it felt like a mostly useless piece of information amid my flood of unmanageable symptoms, valuable only for being an actual positive test after so many not-quite-enough-bands results for Lyme itself. But eventually my symptoms began to crystallize a bit—instead of agony in my shoulder or my groin or my foot, it would be a region in my shoulder, a single stretch of muscle where my legs met, a chunk of my toe instead of the whole digit. As this change happened, I began to notice when certain regions responded to particular treatments, which pains flared up if a particular antibiotic dropped out of my regimen, and to see in the differing physiological responses indicators that the two infections, Lyme and *Bartonella,* were distributed differently within my body.

So the pain in my hips, my shoulders, my temples—that was probably *Bartonella,* because it would flare up terribly when I stopped taking rifampin, a *Bartonella*-specific antibiotic, and then die back down if I resumed. The pain in my digestive tract, the throat-closing feeling, the vibration in my chest, the old phantom heart attacks—all of that was good old Lyme, to be fought with tetracycline or doxycycline or amoxicillin, plus the panoply of bactericidal herbs. Those pains and others responded to the cyst busters; the regions with *Bartonella* did not.

None of this was clear at the beginning, when I was powerless against the sickness: Once I gained some power, some measure of control, the patterns and predictabilities gradually emerged into the light. So even as I accepted my identity as a sick person, I became *less* mysterian about my condition, and all the pains and problems in my flesh. Acceptance was important, but the work that followed acceptance, seeking not only coexistence but a cure, was a work of reason as much as intuition, intellectual and physical effort rather than a farewell to arms.

BUT THE NATURE OF THAT WORK, OVER MONTHS AND THEN more than months of repetition and experiment, also made it clearer than ever why the Lyme consensus persisted, why official knowledge resisted the kinds of treatments that the Maverick and others were offering, the help that so many patients sought. Because if the rules of modern medicine demand replicability and simplicity in treatment, plus a strong dose of "first, do no harm" caution in dosages and duration, then what I had embarked upon was *way* outside those bounds, and it was hard to imagine how my experience could be translated into a prescription that was testable and replicable along the lines that official medicine requires.

Those studies of so-called long-term IV courses, for instance, that supplied the supposed clincher for the case against extending antibiotic treatment for chronic Lyme—they were short-term trifles compared with what I was doing, with my months and months and still more months of multiple antibiotics, my ever-expanding and ever-changing battery of herbs and enzymes, to say nothing of my reckless pet-store dosing on the side. If those studies were the maximum that official medicine would consider, if six or eight weeks of treatment pushed the limits of controlled trials and gold-standard results, then how could you even *imagine* a study that tested the kind of treatment I was pursuing, cobbling together, inventing? (Then, too, when I tried to envision a longitudinal study that set out to test even the simplest version of what I was doing, all I could think about was the chronic Lyme patients on the placebo, sentenced to two years of false hope and permanent misery in the name of scientific inquiry.)

Meanwhile, if anything was clear from reading the literature or talking to doctors and their patients, it was that every chronic case of Lyme disease had to be beaten or mitigated in a different way. In *Cure Unknown,* Pamela Weintraub recounts how her family of four were all infected in the same yard, the same woods, the same neighborhood—and yet she, her husband, and their two sons followed completely variable paths toward recovery. *Nine months to a year,* the Maverick told new patients who asked how long he typically treated—but by the time I had spent a year of my own life in his care, I realized that this average concealed a ridiculous range, from people who walked about feeling better after five or ten weeks to recalcitrant cases who might be pulsing antibiotics for three years. Or forever: A low-dose "maintenance" regime, for someone who felt 90 percent better but whose symptoms still recurred a few days a month or a few hours a day, was a pretty commonplace endgame for the harder cases. What would it mean to study *that?*

"I just want to be able to give my patients a normal prescription," the Maverick said to me wearily in one of our conversations. "*Take this for six weeks and you'll feel better.* And someday, we'll find something that works like that. But until then, as a doctor, I have to find the thing that makes you feel better—however long it takes."

I also realized over time that he and many of his colleagues were influenced not just by what they saw in their patients, what seemed to work in their practices, but by some formative personal experience that awakened them to the reality of chronic Lyme. The Maverick had become a Lyme doctor because his father, apparently dying of congestive heart failure, was given a strong dose of antibiotics and recovered to live for decades more: It was Lyme carditis, undiagnosed. A nurse practitioner he sometimes worked with, who specialized in IV vitamin C, did so because that had been the key to her own recovery, after spending her entire twenties sick. Another local Lyme specialist had been turned on to her preferred treatments when her husband was diagnosed with Lou Gehrig's disease, the always fatal ALS, but then tested positive for Lyme and slowly recovered under her care. (That Lou Gehrig himself owned a summer house near Old Lyme is a detail that sticks in the mind.) A scholar working on chronic Lyme at a major New York university had a wife who had spent years undiagnosed and who couldn't bear sunlight because of the damage Lyme had done to her eyes.

So the doctors were like their patients. Each was an N of 1, each had some personal story behind their migration toward the fringe, and many had been forced to accept the reality of chronic Lyme by a direct or familial experience that left no other choice.

But if this created a bond between patients and doctors, it also widened the separation between the Lyme doctors and their mainstream counterparts—many of whom, like my family physician, had their own milder experiences that made the consensus seem solid, the dissenting views implausible. Because if everything was inevitably personal, and if the main path from one team to another involved some kind of doubting-Thomas moment, where the reality of chronic Lyme was confirmed in your own flesh or a loved one's suffering—well, then the fundamental conflict seemed that much more intractable, that much harder for mere research and debate to overcome.

Let me offer a note of optimism, though. If there is one thing that makes the chronic-Lyme world different from other realms of alternative or outsider medicine, it's the centrality of antibiotics, a paradigmatic insider-approved treatment, to its preferred cure. Often in medical debates the pattern is reversed: The establishment recommends antibiotics, the outsiders and mavericks worry that they're overpre-scribed, the holistic types warn about their side effects. But with Lyme it's the establishment that retreats to mystery, while the dissenters are yelling about how we already have the necessary drugs.

For all that long-term treatment layers on supplements and herbs and strange hypotheses, its foundation is still a medical standby, and its practitioners rarely reject the core modern theory of how to fight infection. And this points, or at least gestures, toward a potential synthesis between estab-lished medicine and its critics. In one of the more famous studies that supposedly showed the folly of alternative medi-cal treatments, published in 2018 in *The Journal of the Ameri-can Medical Association,* cancer patients who reported using complementary or alternative treatments were more likely to die than patients who simply followed the approved chemo-and-radiation track. But they were more likely to die be-cause while taking the alternative medicines they were also more likely to halt the conventional treatment—suggesting that the major peril of experimenting outside the medical consensus is that you become so skeptical, you stop recogniz-ing basic things the establishment gets right.

This is a peril that chronic-Lyme treatment mostly avoids. For all its complexity, its mix of grim persistence and strange speculation, it's still attached at the root to the most basic and commonplace prescriptions. And through all of my own bat-tles, through every strange internet-recommended thing I tried, I always knew that antibiotics were the infantry in my internal warfare, the forces whose initial landing had made this a real battle rather than just a dismal, bloody rout.

. . .

But to extend that metaphor a final time, there could be no victory if the body itself couldn't rally and generate infantry and defenses of its own. Here Sontag's scornful invocation of colonial wars was actually quite apt. The antibiotics and everything else I threw into the battle were fundamentally outsiders to the country, no more native to my body than U.S. grunts in Vietnam, and the enemy was dug in pretty deep. "We can't turn your body into a sterile environment," one doctor told me, unconsciously echoing a thousand critics of scorched-earth campaigning. "You can kill bacteria with antibiotics, but they'll always come back unless your own system can keep them in check."

At a certain point, after endless effort with antibiotics and cyst busters, I began to feel something like that—a feeling that was strange at first, even frightening, before I realized that it had to be my own suppressed immune system grinding back to life. (There was a flood of relief and recognition when the kids brought home one of their innumerable colds and I suffered a bout of normal congestion—my first in more than two years.) What that meant, at first, was that I began to have Herxheimer reactions without drugs: If I induced stronger symptoms with herbs or just felt them bubbling up, the ache or dissociation in my joints and muscles would expand a certain distance before it was met with an itching, rubbing, Herxheimerish response, followed by the characteristic relaxation and exhaustion. All this without having taken any antibiotics; all this seemingly generated by my immune system alone.

So I began, at last, after about a year, to slowly taper my insane regimen of drugs. Where once I felt like I had to take an antibiotic every few hours to prevent the symptoms from overwhelming everything, I now found I could take them only every six hours, and on good days that meant just a handful—three or four instead of the twelve pills or more I took at my peak. If I tapered too fast, the symptoms still came back, as though my immune system were a half-trained local force easily overwhelmed by experienced guerrillas. But over more months of experiments, I slowly dropped my dosage to just a few small pills a day.

This alone made an important change in my everyday existence. Alongside the pain itself, in this period there was an obsessive thinking *about* treatments—what herb to take next, whether I was ready for another antibiotic dose, did I have enough pills in my back pocket to get me through an afternoon—that permeated every workday, every family meal, every car trip. So just to have that obsession drop away a little was a victory, a sign that I was actually getting somewhere on my long, slow crawl.

Around this time we went with our kids to a summertime picnic, the kind that runs late into the evening, where the girls ran around with other children with dirty faces while their brother toddled after them. As we gathered our family up to take them all home, I realized that I had spent two hours in adult conversation, punctuated by occasional child wrangling, without thinking about my next pill—a milestone that I remember to this day.

My dreams began to change, too. They were the same kinds of dreams—about vast and drafty houses, antique libraries or Gothic banks, spaces that outside invaders had somehow entered, to lurk in hidden wings and pools of shadow. But something different happened just before I woke, when it came time for the enemy to actually appear—in masked faces, zombie grins, vampiric leers.

I was still terrified by their appearance, still rooted to the spot. But there were other characters in my dreamscape now, with their own agency and purposes. And I'll never forget the early morning when—just before I woke to a frantic itching feeling all over my head—a librarian suddenly popped up from behind a marble counter and shot one of the vampires in the face.

6

Excavations

OVER THE PERIOD I'VE JUST DESCRIBED—ABOUT A YEAR'S worth of treatment, from the fall of 2016 to the fall of 2017—we must have shown our home to prospective buyers thirty times. It was a chaotic process, racing through the rooms to pick up scattered toys and domestic detritus, frantically scrubbing a smear of baby food off the kitchen countertops, making sure the diaper pail was emptied, the girls' beds all made up, the piles of books returned to their shelves, and—of course—all my pill bottles swept from the bedside into my secret storage spaces, my bathroom drawer and desk. Then we'd race to the minivan, the kids piled in, the baby strapped down, and away, driving to a park or a grandparent's house or even Costco—the whole thing an act of hope, a rehearsal for the day we might leave the house for good.

Returning after the showing was always painful, especially for Abby. We would come back and encounter the house in its pristine form, as we wanted others to see it, as we had once seen it ourselves. And we would encounter all the changes we'd made—the new garden outside, the repaired patios and fences, and above all everything my wife had done inside, before and after the baby, the decorating that made the sunroom splendid with rattan couches and a splintered country table, the dining room curtained and book-lined, the living room with its Revolutionary-era fireplace a cozy scene out of a *Country Living* magazine. It was a photo-shoot vision of the life we had imagined ourselves making, the house as Abby had conceived it—and now we had to accept that all our work was wasted and simply give it up.

Except that nobody wanted to take it. Despite all the money we'd invested in improvements, despite how fine it looked in the summer light and autumn color, despite the sunny confidence of the agents swooping in to take house hunters around, the home just sat and sat and sat.

I had feared something like this when Trump won his unexpected victory. Late that night, while everyone else in Punditland processed the shocking implications for our politics, I sat slumped on the living room couch, staring up at the long exposed beam that dipped a little where the house had settled, thinking about the stock market drop that was widely expected if Trump somehow won.

Now we'll never get out of this fucking house, I thought.

The crash didn't happen; the pundits were wrong yet again. Instead, exactly when we put the house on the market, the stock market surged. Yet it made no difference to our desperate search for a buyer.

So it wasn't Trump's fault that we were stuck. In part it was just localized ill luck: A major employer in a nearby town had shifted its headquarters from the Connecticut suburbs to Boston shortly after we made our purchase, and the sudden exodus of upper-middle-class professionals created a glut of expensive houses that dragged everybody down. In part it was the general decline of suburban and exurban prices as fewer millennials, relative to prior generations, married and bought homes.

But in part it was just our own amazing folly. We had imagined ourselves buying a "forever home" (now a terrifying phrase, evocative of *You've always been the caretaker, Mr. Torrance*), and we had felt fortunately flush with cash, so our negotiations had not included the most rigorous comparisons to nearby homes, or any real attempt to assess whether the eccentricities we loved about the house, its age and rambling property, might be serious impediments to resale. It was enough that the previous owners had dropped the price a lot; surely that showed we were getting a bargain! Honestly, we had felt sorry for them—the idiotic pity that spoiled youth feels for age—and imagined that we were somehow doing them a kindness by accepting their final counter instead of trying to squeeze them to take a little less. (In our defense, or at least mine, the sickness was already at work by the time we reached the last stage of negotiations, and my memory of my thought process is a fog.)

For our folly we were repaid. The house sat on the market all spring; we dropped the price; it sat some more. We dropped it again, below what we had paid for it, and further still, in increments of fifty thousand dollars every six months. Every time we did it we had a conversation about whether we could afford it, and the answer for a while was yes, in the sense that the neighborhoods that we were looking at in New Haven had houses that were much cheaper than our rural retreat. As long as we sold this house for two-thirds of the price we'd paid, we'd still have enough for a new down payment. But in terms of the money we'd invested in the house, to say nothing of our savings for college or retirement, it was a total financial irrationality.

Yet if you were inside our lives, it still made sense. We had lashed our remaining hopes to the promise of escape, and our misery was so entangled with the landscape that to give up on selling and departing would have meant giving up on happiness entirely—as if *The Shining* ended with Wendy Torrance wandering back into a still-standing Overlook and settling in for a century with the ghosts. Our marriage, our family life, our very psychological survival depended on leaving this place no matter what that leaving cost.

So leave we did: In the fall of 2017, with the house still unsold and our finances surviving only because of the brisk sales of Abby's book, we found a rental in New Haven and moved there, exactly two years to the week after our arrival in Connecticut. But *moved* is not quite the right word: We crash-landed, our furniture left behind, our clothes in heaps, our kids baffled, my mother-in-law despairing at what we were thinking, what kind of cliff her son-in-law had dragged her daughter toward.

The rental house was in a lovely neighborhood with friendly landlords who had ascended into university housing at Yale, so we were not exactly moving to the moon. But we still felt like squatters, camping out with their battered-from-years-of-family-life Ikea furniture, trying to keep tabs on the luxury home we still owned that now sat echoing and uninhabited. In this effort we were unsuccessful: A pipe in the vacant house's sunroom burst spectacularly at Christmastime, even as the furnace in our rental house suddenly expired. So we spent that holiday season huddled around space heaters in house 2 even as, in house 1, filthy water pooled and froze across the floors. Every month I made two payments: rent and mortgage. Every month I thought, *This can't go on.* Every month it did.

All this was possible only because of privilege, of course. We were borrowing from my father on top of our own professional-class earnings, and I was fortunate enough to have the kind of job that I could do without having to rise early and commute to an office, and indeed without seeing anyone at all on the days when I was incapable of normal human contact. Had I been a lawyer or a doctor, or for that matter just a different kind of journalist—a real reporter rather than a pontificator—I would have lost my job and we would have simply gone under in the first year of my collapse.

This relative good fortune was hard to appreciate in the utter depths, when I would have traded any amount of money for even a pittance of improvement, but it became more meaningful as I made my glacial sort of progress. And with a sense of my own relative luck came the further realization of just how much doom this kind of disease could deliver. If I was so badly off, with the cushion of savings to pay for treatment, the ability to earn money from home, and the perfect skill set to sift the internet for help, how many people were simply lost from the beginning—consigned to unemployment and isolation, with both treatment and knowledge held cruelly beyond their reach? There was no way to know for sure, but I could guess roughly in my head: If 400,000 cases of Lyme a year yielded 50,000 chronic cases, and if even only a few thousand of those were as bad as mine, then, over the accumulated years, tens of thousands of people had to be facing impossible challenges without the moneyed, highly educated advantages that helped us, barely, to survive.

Still, even upper-middle-class privilege has its limits. At some point our cash flow would turn permanently negative, and our two-house problem would have to be resolved. We tried to rent the country house ("The rental market is hot," our agent promised, as she had once promised us *agricultural exemptions*); there were no takers. We cut the price again; a few showings, nothing more. Finally we fired our sleek realtors and hired in their place a garrulous old town fixture who spun yarns about selling houses for mobsters and remembered doing deals with my wife's father during his own descent.

It was not an ideal omen, but soon after we hired him we did, at last, receive an offer—a ridiculous lowball, an insult, hundreds of thousands below what we had paid three years earlier.

Immediately we accepted, letting all the money we'd earned from our D.C. house's appreciation officially evaporate, letting all our marital savings go with it. We accepted and counted ourselves lucky to get out.

Except the land would not let us go. In our own illness-shadowed negotiations to buy the house, we—or our lawyer, or someone somewhere who was supposed to be responsible—had let a few things go, like some permit problems related to the guest cottage, plus an ancient record of the removal of a fuel tank buried on the property. Our buyers were not so blithe or hapless, they didn't feel sorry for us in the slightest, and the husband was particularly hard-nosed. So the things we needed to do to close the deal multiplied, and our garrulous realtor had to pull all his local strings, setting us up with the town officials we needed to expedite our easement application, and with the professional fixer whose entire job seemed to be to handle these kinds of situations, where stupid home buyers from the city bought without due diligence and couldn't get out again without his help.

The fixing was the easy part. The soil test for the long-abandoned fuel tank yielded some *anomalies*—as it happened, in exactly the zone where I had dug and then filled in the hole to pipe gas to our generator—and so we had to do some light excavation. This, unfortunately, turned up yet another fuel tank not so far away, very much unremoved, its metal partially rusted away and God knows what spilled out into the soil. The workmen hauled it out, their rueful pity evident, on a chilly morning early in the spring, and I stood over it in a heavy coat, staring at the tangle of metal and old roots, which looked for all the world like a giant burrowing insect hauled up into the light.

It was all too much, I thought, driving back to New Haven, and then back and forth and back and forth again, to supervise the tests, the digging, the sampling, the further tests, the thousands of dollars in costs turning into tens of thousands, the land as poisoned as my body, the feeling of contamination confirmed by a liquid darkness in the earth itself.

We couldn't just leave. We had to dig ourselves out.

AT THIS POINT EXCAVATION WAS ALSO THE THEME OF MY medical experiments. Overall I had reached a new kind of equilibrium. The pain was still there, the symptomology hadn't left, and it still felt like there was *wrongness* in every joint and muscle group. But the degree of pain was usually much milder than in the first two years, a discomfort rather than an agony. The brain fog had mostly departed, the mental anguish diminished markedly, and my ability to do normal things—converse or eat or watch a TV show without my symptoms crowding in—had partially returned. On one or two days out of seven I felt something recognizable as happiness or pleasure or optimism; another two or three I felt robotic but okay; and only about a third of my days were lost to pain and pessimism the way six or seven days a week had been lost when I was at my worst.

Peeling an onion was a common metaphor in Lyme circles for the treatment I'd been doing, the courses of antibiotics meeting layer upon layer of symptoms—plus, of course, the accompanying tears. But the image that always came into my mind was from C. S. Lewis's *The Voyage of the Dawn Treader,* in which an unpleasant boy named Eustace Clarence Scrubb is transformed into a dragon by his own avarice and then invited by Aslan, the Christ figure, to bathe in a healing pool.

Except that he's told that first he must undress, which he realizes means tearing off his outer scales—casting his skin as a snake might. So he scratches and finds that the whole skin comes off easily, "beautifully, like it does after an illness, or as if I was a banana." Then, happily, he goes down to the pool to bathe—except just as he's about to put his feet in the water he looks down and sees that "they were all hard and rough and wrinkled and scaly just as they had been before." So he scratches again and tears off the next layer, and the next, and each time he goes to the water and still sees a dragon staring back at him.

Finally the lion speaks: "You will have to let me undress you." Eustace realizes that means using his claws, which is terrifying, but not as frightening as remaining in the dragon's form. So he lets Aslan do it: "The very first tear he made was so deep that I thought it had gone right into my heart. And when he began pulling the skin off, it hurt worse than anything I've ever felt. The only thing that made me able to bear it was just the pleasure of feeling the stuff peel off." Soon the skin is on the ground beside him, a huge, dark, knobby thing, and the lion takes him and throws him in the water. Swimming around, he realizes, with joy and relief, "I'd turned into a boy again."

The problem was that I didn't have a lion to help me—though not for want of asking. As I kept peeling and peeling, my dragon-ness shrunk and my human self showed through. But always the scales were still there—patches now instead of a full coat, but enough armor to keep me locked into ill health.

Moreover, the scales could still expand again if my human body showed any weakness. The immune response was there to help me, at long last, but anything that stressed my immune system seemed to bring the bad days back. A head cold would mean three days of normal congestion and then fifteen days of resurgent Lyme symptoms in my cranium. A bout of stomach flu would leave my intestinal tract inflamed, the old gagging and diarrhea back, for weeks after the fever and nausea of the primary infection passed. Likewise with other difficulties, other forms of weakness. When I sprained my ankle playing basketball, in addition to the pain of the injury there were symptoms up and down my damaged leg. I had never been allergic to insect bites, but when a wasp stung me on my right hand while I was raking leaves, I had several days of swelling and itching on the bitten hand, and then a bizarre week where the Lyme symptoms surged but only on my right-hand side.

So *it* was there, still there, still armored underneath, and I had to find ways to push claws into the chinks. My ill-fated basketball game was one such attempt at excavation: Once I found myself capable of even minimal exercise, I also found that anything that moved a given muscle group aggressively could stir up whatever lay hidden in my tissue, giving me extra symptoms for a time and then, usually, improvement. When I went swimming, my arms burned overnight. When I bought a bicycle and started riding, there was an immediate surge of symptoms, less in my legs than in my groin, where the seat put pressure on the tissue of my nether regions. Every new form of exercise guaranteed a flare of pain and sometimes more.

The same flares happened when I did things to try to relax my muscles: osteopath and chiropractor visits, doses of CBD oil. (Alas, I never graduated to marijuana.) I also flared up from a new set of supplements and herbs, with strange names like terminalia chebula and N-acetylcysteine, which came recommended by doctors and Lyme forums alike, because they promised to dissolve the biofilms in which multiple kinds of bacteria could bond and network and hide. Over time these became the major supplements I took, along with my now-reduced antibiotic load. I dug and stripped, dug and stripped, all the while believing that there was a healthy person underneath.

The Maverick was less certain. He was pleased with my gains and took notes on my experiments even when they frustrated him, but he grew exasperated when I would come in for appointments and report that in the previous three months the symptoms in, say, my wrist had improved by 3 percent, so that instead of being 85 percent well I was 88 percent well . . .

"I'm a little worried that you're living out Zeno's paradox here," he said to me one day. "You know, the one where someone goes half the distance, and then half the distance again, and never actually gets there. You could be subdividing your symptoms like this indefinitely."

I shook my head. The slowness of my progress was absurd, but I still felt sure that there was progress. And as long as there was progress, there could be an ending, a final victory, health regained.

"Okay," he said, "but I have to tell you, with the hardest cases—and at this point you know you're a hard case; I'm not saying anything you don't know—I see a lot of patients who get a *lot* better, who get their lives back, who can work and be happy and basically live what looks like normal life, even though something's still in there, even though they're always at 90 percent, not 100 percent. And sometimes you have to treat *getting better* as the big victory, even if you don't get completely *well*."

Then he revealed to me that he might be one of those patients himself. His father's carditis had been a gateway into Lymeworld, but a few years before I found my way to his clinic the Maverick had been graced with his own tick-borne illness, which resisted every treatment and left him bedridden and immobilized, his practice suspended for two years, until finally he worked his way to the revelation that he had brucellosis—an infection of the joints and muscles, usually contracted through bad meat or milk but sometimes carried (like so many wonderful things) by the humble deer tick.

He had restored himself, over a year of treatment with multiple antibiotics, to the point where he could live normally and work as a doctor once again. But the man who greeted me when I staggered, dazed and hopeless, into his office in the fall of 2015 wasn't actually healthy himself. And the man reacting skeptically to my reports of tiny increments of progress in what was now early 2018 was still sometimes symptomatic, still sometimes taking drugs, still experimenting— still, like me, in pain.

It was a startling moment, this revelation about a man I'd seen every few months for almost three years, and whose persona throughout was brusquely analytical, data-driven, impatient, and intense—the scholar of illness, not the sufferer. Not just the realization that he was carrying pain, but the thought of how many other lives he had been able to help save, my own included, because he had found a way to save himself.

"So I have to ask," he said as I processed all this, "how would you feel if you had to live the rest of your life this way? Could you do it?"

I shook my head. I was proving, day by day, that the answer was yes. But I still could not bring myself to entertain the question.

THE CONTAMINATED SOIL FINALLY CAME OUT, AFTER TEN thousand dollars' worth of sampling and digging. There was enough of it to fill an envelope, at most. But by now I knew just how tiny a dose it takes to poison an entire system.

So we moved at last toward closing. In those final weeks, the cloud of dread and paranoia returned to me as I waited for some last crisis to intervene, some grasping hand to reach up from the soil and hold us there. The beam in the living room ceiling with the sag in it became a particular fixation, and every time I visited the house I found myself staring at it, imagining that it had settled a little more since the last visit, that it was buckling or cracking, that some structural disaster loomed.

In truth it was stable and unmoving, with multiple inspections attesting to its solidity. The house's actual last gasp was much smaller: On the day of the buyers' walk-through, they found the oven broken, for no particular reason save perhaps disuse, and so we had one final day-of-closing negotiation where they pried an extra thousand dollars out of us.

Then it was finished. For our finances, the deal was a catastrophe. For our lives, our marriage, it was the narrowest of escapes.

The new owners are hunters. I think they might actually shoot the deer.

SOME PART OF ME, THE STORYTELLING PART, HOPED THAT MY symptoms would depart once the house was sold—that, having divested ourselves of our prideful mistake, we would be rewarded with relief; that, having accepted Providence's shove onto a different path, we would find the way suddenly smoothed.

That didn't happen. The peeling, the slow exfoliation, the excavation continued as before. But my relationship with New England did change for the better. Once we were planted in the city again, once we bought a new house with an enclosed backyard and sidewalks all around, the countryside became tolerable again.

On weekends, we would drive with the kids deep into the Connecticut country, up the old roads that I remembered from my youth. Looking out at the fields and forests, I no longer felt the loathing for the landscape that I had felt in the depths of my imprisonment. Some days I could almost recall the attraction I once felt to white-shingled houses standing in tall grass, to red barns buried in forsythia, to a meadow of one's own, to the romance of the land.

But I was still looking at these vistas from a distance, with a bottle of pills still pressing in my hip pocket. And always I could see what lay behind them—the woods and their darkness, cool and enveloping and deep.

7

Where the Ladders Start

THERE IS A VERSION OF THIS BOOK THAT DOESN'T IN-
clude this chapter, and for a certain kind of reader it
might be the better book to read. I want this account to be
helpful to the cause of chronic Lyme patients, and to anyone
working on the frontiers of medicine or suffering from
chronic illness. I hope to convince the skeptical reader that
the case for the persistence of Lyme disease is powerful, and
that the regimens prescribed by Lyme specialists represent a
reasonable and empirical response to an extremely knotty
problem. I don't want readers to come away from my account
thinking that chronic disease of any kind is just a mystery, a
mind-body phenomenon beyond scientific ken. Which means
that I want to present myself as a fundamentally reliable nar-
rator, open-minded but not naïve, vulnerable but not an
outright wreck, aware of my own limitations and the possible doubts about my story, but neither paranoid nor mad.

But I also want to tell a true story, and that means going
a little further into the medical borderlands, deeper into the
stranger aspects of my own bodily experience. So that's what
this chapter is for, separated from the main narrative so that

it can be read independently—though it will bleed into the final chapters, and its revelations are part of what I've brought with me back up out of the dark. Still, readers who find these parts of the story hard to credit can know that I sympathize with their reaction, and I hope they find the rest persuasive even so.

LET'S START, THEN, BY TALKING ABOUT THE THINGS THAT people with Lyme disease try that aren't just long-term antibiotics supplemented with herbs and enzymes, but a bit more unusual and radical than even that. I can't speak to all such experiments: I have not, for instance, entered the kind of hyperbaric chamber that our medical-supply millionaire friend set up inside his Main Street home, which promises to kill off the anaerobic bacteria by flooding the bloodstream with oxygen; nor ozone therapy, which promises similar results through the simpler medium of an IV.

Nor have I tried to sweat the disease out of my system through the use of a portable sauna for my home, which many long-term patients swear by. I tried acupuncture once or twice early in my journey, the only notable result being an unexpected burst of tears when a needle went in at a spot supposedly associated with emotional blockages. I have never attempted Reiki healing, been treated with bee venom, exposed myself to ultraviolet light or photon therapy, or submitted to colonics.

I have, however, dosed myself extensively with vitamin C, first orally and then with the nurse practitioner I mentioned earlier, who offered IV treatment in an annex of her Westport home. She was a fascinating example of how the

intersection of a suburban illness with suburban money cre-
ates an aesthetic that you might call Holistic Preppy, blurring
old-fashioned Connecticut privilege with New Age flour-
ishes. Her home was on the same country road where Martha Stewart once kept a house, and she treated patients near
the paddock where she kept her sheep. (For some people, at
least, even Lyme couldn't kill the farming fantasy.) But her
practice was one of the more New Age that I attended, with
crystals on the windowsills and tarot cards decorating the
walls, watching me as I told my story: the Magician and the
Wheel of Fortune, the lightning-struck Tower and the Fool.

The physical experience of the treatment, however, was
straightforward, with no occult emanations. The first few
sessions induced strong Herxheimer reactions, the desire to
move and rub and tap my feet. Then the feeling diminished
and soon I reacted to the infusions barely if at all. (This happened a lot with treatments that were outside the antibiotics-
and-herbs routine: an initially strong reaction, as though
some new layer had been scraped, and then equilibrium
again.)

At that point, the nurse pronounced me cured and congratulated me on my full return to health, which offended
me, since I was not, in fact, restored. But I went back to her
one more time and she couldn't find a vein, and I left stabbed
and uninfused and miserable. Maybe she had intuited the
limits of her treatment, if not the end of the disease itself.

Vitamin C is hardly the weirdest thing that one might
take, of course. There is plenty of research suggesting that it
acts as a support and restorative for the immune system,
which is why just about everyone takes it for the common
cold, and there's a lively debate about the effectiveness of IV
treatment for severe conditions like sepsis. It's generally con-

sidered safe, and even somewhat *normal,* by doctors skeptical of other Lyme treatments.

A more eccentric supplement was capsuled salt, which is part of a "salt protocol" for Lyme disease, available in a three-ring binder from Amazon.com, that I briefly attempted when I was near my worst. At that point it didn't seem to offer any benefit. But years later, when I began taking the biofilm-dissolving substances in large quantities, theoretically releasing more and more bacteria into my bloodstream, I found myself absolutely craving salt, which I took in big white capsules, like bullets of dried ocean water, while also devouring potato chips, Doritos, peanuts, Asian soups. I never visited a salt cave, a supposedly healing space that's cropped up in various unlikely storefronts around the state, but my insides might have wanted one: There was a period of two weeks when I ate sodium-heavy Vietnamese broths for every single meal, driving around the suburbs of New Haven to vary the restaurants where I lunched, ordering the same pho for breakfast, lunch, and dinner. Again, after about a month of my salt fixation, equilibrium and a more normal appetite returned.

Around this same time, while we were living in New Haven but still trying to sell the country house, I began corresponding occasionally with other chronic Lyme patients, usually when a friend put us in touch, thinking that I might be a helpful resource, since by now I could talk like an authority on the subject of the illness and its treatments. Just as often, they had something interesting to offer me: For instance, a woman from Texas, a friend of a Baylor academic, reported a positive experience with a clinic in Idaho, run by a chiropractor who promised to rid patients of Lyme disease by applying "gentle therapeutic magnets" to the symptomatic areas of their body—a painless, non-invasive therapy that made her feel surprisingly better after a two-week intensive program.

I was not about to go spend a couple of weeks in Idaho, asking Abby to accept the theory of magnetic treatment while I left her with the kids, but there was a chiropractor in central Connecticut who offered a similar treatment, just fifty bucks per appointment, and I thought, *What the hell.* (I thought that a lot about treatments in those days.) So I drove up I-91 one morning after dropping the kids at school and submitted myself to her ministrations, which were really two fringe treatments rolled into one: the magnets themselves and then, to determine exactly where to place them, a little bit of muscle testing, so-called kinesiology, in which the practitioner asks your body questions and gets answers through the resistance, or lack thereof, to her pressure in hands or muscle groups.

The mechanism whereby this theory is supposed to work is not susceptible to normal scientific investigation, suggesting as it does a radically different conception of how the body works—indeed, what the body *is*—than Western medicine accepts. That's the long-winded way of saying that to a reasonable American M.D., kinesiology is on a similar plane as magic. And I consider myself a reasonable patient, which is why when I tell you that the Magnetizer had a pretty impressive success rate—80 percent at least—using this method to identify (without my telling her) the places where I was feeling particularly symptomatic on any given day, I don't expect you to believe this was any more than coincidence, supplemented by the power of suggestion.

The magnets themselves, on the other hand, do have a little bit of research behind them, albeit mostly studies on the effects of magnetic fields on microorganisms in a test tube, not bacteria buried deep in flesh. ("The ability of bacteria to form colonies decreased with increasing magnetic field intensity and with increasing time of exposure . . .") So maybe it's less of a leap for the skeptical reader to accept that the first time I lay on her table, in a darkened room for half an hour, with flat magnets taped to about fifteen places around my body, it didn't take long before the old familiar jerking, rubbing, flailing feeling kicked in, as though *something* was happening in the flesh and muscle beneath the flat metal disks.

Lying on that table week after week, in the back end of a mostly derelict strip mall, while the rest of the Magnetizer's patients—normal chiropracty patients, on average twice my age—shuffled and murmured in adjoining rooms gave me a lot of time to ponder the deep questions: *How did I get here? What would my 2015 self say if he could see me now? Do other columnists do things like this? Did Walter Lippmann ever get magnetized? How about Tom Friedman?*

Sometimes the Herxheimer feeling continued once I had made my way back outside, into the empty parking lot, catty-corner from a diner just called DINER, and I would do a few jumping jacks in the abandoned bank drive-through or stand rubbing my neck in front of the one-way mirror on the optometrist's window, wondering if anyone was staring at me from inside.

Once, a flurry of snow began to fall as I stood there, pale in the heavy "dad coat" that Abby had procured for the Connecticut winters, my hair standing up in tufts around my bald spot, thinking about how I had fallen into this pit as a still-young man and would be scrabbling out, assuming I ever did, as a definite inhabitant of middle age.

But honestly, I enjoyed these trips, the feeling of being at the opposite end of the Lyme social spectrum from my Martha Stewart–meets–the–tarot excursions. There was no pressure in the Magnetizer's office to be anything but another creaking sick person, a younger version of the seventy-somethings who visited her for their constant aches and pains. The experience of being physically handled had its own grace, independent of whatever else it accomplished. And I liked her: She was the New England version of a Russian grandmother, short and square and quick-talking, with big glasses beneath her bun of hair and an ageless cast to her complexion.

She believed in lots of things, of course: not just the magnets or the kinesiology or the herbs she recommended when I showed up with a cold, but the kind of conspiracy-coded things whose mere mention my prior self would have taken as a reason to tune out everything else she had to say. (*Well, of course, people out west have to deal with getting sick from chemtrails,* she might say during a discussion of the pros and cons of living in New England.)

My new self, though, regarded her radical openness rather differently—as a feature of the kind of mind that was more likely than the rest of us to grope its way to veiled or disreputable truths. Give that feature too much freedom, too much rein, and you would end up with a purely conspiratorial worldview, impervious to contrary facts, ready to throw out vaccination or refuse chemotherapy. But exclude such openness entirely and you end up with the mindset that I had encountered across my months of frustration, where the absence of an exact test result matching a set of bureaucratic criteria meant that doctor after doctor would spread their hands, hint that you were crazy, and abandon you to pain.

So I didn't become a chemtrails believer in her care, or

imagine that her worldview could simply substitute for official medical knowledge. But without some element of her
open-to-all-theories attitude, the progress of science becomes the recitation of consensus. And for someone like me,
for whom that recitation had been a closed door in my face,
her existence was a gift.

BUT LONG BEFORE I WENT TO THE MAGNETIZER'S OFFICE, I
had brought an even stranger treatment into our home, setting it up on my desk like an invention in some *Twilight Zone*
episode, a mystery box with dials and numbers waiting for
some luckless character to turn it on.

In my first months of illness, I tried to distinguish myself
from those other sick people, more desperate than I was,
who were trying truly crazy things while I was proceeding
sensibly and moderately along the path to health. *I'm bad but
not that bad,* I would think when people told me about taking
months of IV antibiotics—until, of course, I took IV antibiotics myself. *I'm bad but not that bad,* I would think while
walking through the chronic-Lyme photograph exhibit in
the local library, with its pictures of patients with their pla-
toons of pill bottles, dozens or hundreds lined up in rows—
until, of course, I found myself with drawers full of enough
pill bottles to put those medicine cabinets to shame. *I'm bad
but not that bad,* I would think while I sat in a waiting room
reading about some exotic treatment—until, of course, I
found myself going in for that treatment myself.

That was where the Rife machine came from. It was the
thing I wouldn't try, because I wasn't crazy, and it cost a
thousand dollars that we needed for the generator or the

curtain drain—until the second year of my illness, still in the country house, when I finally allowed my father to purchase one as what passed for a present in that phase of my life.

The name came from Royal Raymond Rife, a striking name for a very American character, an inventor who worked on several kinds of microscopes and then achieved brief renown in the 1930s and '40s for claiming to have discovered a "mortal oscillatory rate" for various pathogens, a sound frequency at which they would vibrate and then shatter, much like a wineglass exposed to the pitch of a skillful opera singer. This discovery was, alas, suppressed by powerful medical interests, which claimed to have discredited both his results and his machine but really had just "brainwashed and intimidated" his colleagues—or so Rife claimed, on his way to a death in poverty and obscurity in 1971.

His work was exhumed the following decade, in a book with the arresting title *The Cancer Cure That Worked,* whose author claimed that a well-designed "Rife machine" could rid the body of cancerous cells, if only the corrupt medical establishment would allow it to be used. Soon such frequency generators were in wide circulation, sold with booklets that offered an ever-expanding list of sound frequencies that supposedly matched up with different ailments, from the most obscure bacteria and parasites to the common cold. These were often peddled in multilevel marketing schemes, with sketchy claims that the FDA had approved them "for investigational purposes" and endorsements from "research institutes" that were just fronts for the salesmen. The caliber of person drawn to this work can perhaps be inferred from the case of a particularly successful saleswoman named Kimberly Bailey, a California woman whose career as a Rife machine entrepreneur was cut short when she was sentenced to life in prison in 2002 for plotting the kidnapping, torture, and murder of her business partner and lover, one Richard Post III, at the hands of hitmen in Tijuana.

When I read up on Rife machines online, outside of Lyme disease forums, these were the stories I immediately encountered—the purest quackery, unfiltered snake oil. Yet as with the magnets, there were also hints in the scientific literature that some version of Rife's theory was possibly correct. Electromagnetic frequencies have been shown to reduce tumor growth, for instance, and some electromagnetic field machines have been approved by the FDA for treating certain cancers. (Interestingly, there's also a lot of fear, in holistic circles, of what electromagnetic fields might do to people; the panic over 5G, for instance, reverses the hopeful theories about electromagnetism.) The literature on audio frequencies is more limited, but in 2016 a team of researchers in Georgia succeeded in using "sonication," the application of high-level sound frequencies, to kill off *E. coli* in goat meat. The mechanism was the same one claimed by Rife: The high frequency's wave energy shook the bacterial cells apart.

Then there was the anecdata: the thousands of Lyme patients who swore by the machines, who claimed to have made gains using them that no antibiotic treatment had achieved. *The New Yorker*'s 2013 "Lyme Wars" investigation, for instance, began with the case of Kaleigh Ahern, a Saratoga Springs collegian who spent eight months on antibiotics after a tick bite and bull's-eye rash led to crippling headaches, burning muscles, insomnia—the whole familiar catalog. Seeing no improvement on the drugs, she switched to a regimen of dietary changes and treatments with a Rife machine— which led to a gradual (albeit incomplete) recovery, allowing her to graduate from college and become a tick researcher herself. The writer, a fine science journalist, took Ahern's story seriously: "She knows that her approach to Lyme disease is controversial and acknowledges that the improvements might be due to her dietary regimen or to Rife treatments or to a placebo effect. She doesn't mind; after enduring such pain, she has found that fine points don't matter."

That last sentence resonated, if you will, with my own Lyme experience; it was the kind of testimony that finally persuaded me to try the machine myself. It came, as promised, with the thick ringed binder of instructions, whose preamble informed me that "as an American national, you have a legal right to medically treat yourself by common law according to Amendment IX of the U.S. Constitution," along with a disavowal of any claims for specific medical "effects or performances" from the frequencies listed in the book. After that came a lot of advice on the different kinds of sound frequencies generated by the machine (sine waves and square waves, audio and "RF" frequencies), when and whether to use an amplifier, and how to hook up the metal hand cylinders—which were wrapped in terry cloth and, when dampened and gripped, were supposed to transmit the sound waves from the machine into my flesh. The book advised me to drink a lot of water, lest the Herxheimer effect get too overwhelming: "Eight full 8 oz. glasses per day will keep the kidney and bowel systems able to eliminate the toxins without discomfort."

Then came the frequency list itself. First, there were 873 pre-programmed "channels," each combining multiple frequencies, from single digits up to 40,000 hertz, and each linked to a specific ailment, from acidosis to zygomycosis, botulism to bubonic plague. The list ran for eighty pages, and then came one hundred more: the "New CAFL," for "Consolidated Anecdotal Frequency List," which went beyond the frequencies discovered by Rife and his followers to include fifty years' worth of discoveries by ordinary sick people using the machines. "These people have shared these frequencies but no medical claims are made for any of them," the book advised. "Use these frequencies at your own risk."

The preamble felt a bit like being recruited into Scientology, handed an E-Meter, and told that maybe enlightenment awaited but that L. Ron Hubbard Inc. offered no guarantee that it would actually be achieved. The list, though, was something much weirder. Did all the endless numbers, the complex frequency combinations, the treatments for obscure diseases represent the fruits of a multigenerational labor, some kind of secret investigation conducted by the sick and suffering over not just years but decades? It felt like something out of a paranoid fiction, a slice of invented Americana by way of Paul Auster or Thomas Pynchon.

Was it just a hoax? Were the Rife peddlers sitting down at their computers with a random number generator and a copy of the Index of Diseases and Injuries, playing mix and match, relying on the placebo effect to hoodwink the rubes, secure in the knowledge that nobody was ever actually going to fire up the Rife machine to treat, say, Eustachian tube inflammation (channel number 263, recommended frequencies: 1550, 880, 37233, 803, 3614, and half a dozen more)? That was disturbing and depressing, but maybe not as unsettling as the possibility that a real collection of people with Eustachian tube inflammation had compiled these frequencies from their own private experiments, establishing a layer of secret knowledge beneath the shell of quackery.

There were two channels listed for Lyme disease, each

one containing dozens of frequencies, a surplus relative to the rest of the book. The default time for a session was five minutes; the book recommended running the Lyme channels for one minute at a time at first, to see how your body handled it. (By this point I was deep into the reckless self-dosing phase of my treatment, so I assumed I could handle five minutes, at least.) I set the machine up inside the drop-leaf desk in our back bedroom, my office, the most private space that I could find. It was a winter evening, the kids were in bed, Abby was working on the far side of the house. Through the windows I could see the shadows of tree branches under the January moon. I dampened the terry cloth and gripped the cylinders, like a robot recharging his batteries or a videogame player with a control in either hand.

Then I punched in the first channel and hit start.

Naturally, it worked. Indeed, it worked in the most familiar and by this time predictable way: It made me want to move my body in the spots where I had symptoms, to twist my neck and jerk my knees and rub my muscles, just the way I did when I took my herb-and-antibiotic combinations, except much more suddenly and immediately, with no need to wait for anything to hit the bloodstream. If I turned on the channel when my symptoms were mild, the reaction lasted only a few minutes; if I turned it on when I felt lousier, or when I first woke up in the morning, it could last for twenty minutes, setting me dancing like a marionette on the cords that linked the cylinders to the beeping eighties-computer box. As with antibiotics, after a session was over I felt sleepy, weakened, slightly spaced out for a while. Sometimes I craved chocolate. And thirsty—yes, I definitely felt thirsty.

Of course, this was insane, so to the extent that I was able I conducted experiments, trying frequencies for random illnesses to see if they elicited the same effect (they did not), setting up blind experiments where I ran frequencies without knowing if they were for Lyme disease or not (I could always tell).

These experiments were less rigorous than they might have been, because I didn't involve my long-suffering wife, for whom the arrival of the Rife machine was an unwelcome development, suggesting as it did a touch of mania and undercutting my claims to be turning a corner, my promise that I was slowly gaining ground. At some level I knew the machine would have that effect: I had mentioned to Abby the possibility of getting one at various points during our awful IV-antibiotic summer, but I didn't actually tell her when it arrived at my dad's house, or when I carried it unobtrusively up the back stairs to my office. Instead I waited until I had tried it out a few times to mention casually that, by the way, we had a new housemate, about the size of a particularly bulky laptop, that I would be spending a fair amount of time with going forward.

This was not my best marital decision.

"So you're saying you snuck this machine . . . which puts out weird *frequencies* of some kind . . . into our *house*?"

"Well, it doesn't put them out into the air. There are these cylinders—it runs through these cylinders . . ."

In general, Abby's confidence that I was sick with an ailment of the body and that I was really getting better strengthened as I slowly improved. But the machine's presence in our lives—in my country-house office and then in the attic once we reached New Haven—was a condensed symbol of everything she feared about my condition, a reason for her to worry that some of my apparent progress might be built on delusions and placebo-like imaginings.

The reader's reaction may be similar to my wife's, especially since I also have to tell you that it wasn't just the Lyme frequencies that worked. The *Bartonella* frequencies did, too, following the same pattern as my various antibiotics in the different regions they touched. And so did frequencies—not all, but many—that weren't in the book but were passed around on Lyme forums and identified with cyst-busting (840.6 was the crucial one) and biofilms (the catalog was long).

So it wasn't just my improving immune system that enabled me to taper off the antibiotics; the machine helped as well. And with the antibiotics I still took, I found that I could use the frequencies in combination with the drugs, running the cyst-busting frequency or a biofilm frequency and feeling the combination work. I even took it on our vacations, packing it with the portable high chair and the diaper pail, setting it up on splintered tables in the shadowy corner of a rental cottage while my wife watched, and doubted, and didn't mention it at all. Sometimes, when I was trying to go without antibiotics entirely, I brought it into our bedroom, where it remained until Abby ran out of patience—it didn't help that I sometimes forgot to turn it off, letting a faintly sinister buzz permeate our upstairs rooms—and banished it to the attic once again.

The last bit of Rife craziness isn't even about Lyme. At a certain point, as I've mentioned, I began to feel more normal illnesses again, the typical immune response for a cold or stomach bug, those scourges of parents of nursery-school-age kids, spiking up from the thicket of my chronic symptoms and usually making the chronic symptoms worse. Naturally, those illnesses had their own frequencies listed in the book (though the channels for the common cold included a warning: "Mutates constantly: too many strains to include a complete list of sequences"); naturally, I tried them out. And naturally, they did . . . well, something. The head-cold frequencies made my nose hurt and my throat tighten; the frequencies for *E. coli,* which I tried after a bad restaurant experience, made my stomach rumble.

In those cases, the infections passed quickly, so it was tough to say whether running the machine made much of a difference to the course of the disease. If I were to get very speculative, I might guess that *if* the frequencies work, *if* it's not all just my suggestibility meeting successful quackery, then perhaps in some cases they make bacteria vibrate without shattering them, effectively stirring at an infection without doing all that much to kill it off. That's how the Rife frequencies for the cold sometimes made me feel—as though they were poking a nest rather than eradicating it, like the exterminators we hired who could find the ground-wasp nests but couldn't ever quite get rid of them.

But now I'm speculating about what my *feelings* tell me about an unproven treatment with an uncertain mechanism that's associated with charlatans and pyramid schemers. So maybe it's best to shut the drop leaf here over my binder, my metal cylinders, my magical bacteria-killing box.

OVER TIME I CAME TO ASSOCIATE THE RIFE MACHINE AND the magnets with the ending of Yeats's poem "The Circus Animals' Desertion":

> *Now that my ladder's gone*
> *I must lie down where all the ladders start*
> *In the foul rag and bone shop of the heart.*

The phrase "where all the ladders start" evoked an image that was in my mind throughout these years—an image of good health and normalcy as the ground floor of a house, decorated in the bland style of so many HGTV programs, with a big kitchen island and manufactured hardwood floors solidly beneath your feet. (The kind of generically livable suburban house, in other words, that I had snobbishly rejected in favor of our country spread.) Those solid floors were the medical knowledge that every modern person takes for granted, the solid platform of vaccines and diagnostics and treatments that has delivered such unusual physical comfort to our vulnerable race.

When you contract an illness that the medical system can't diagnose or cure, it feels like falling through that floor into the basement underneath. But if you find a group of outside-the-consensus doctors who tell you not to worry, they know what they're doing and there's a good explanation for what's happening to you, then even that basement can seem reassuring—there's a sheetrocked ceiling, a few couches, and a nice workbench to go with the grumbling of furnaces and water tanks, and some paint cans just in case. It's a hidden consensus underneath the official one, maybe not as solid, but strong enough to raise a ladder back to health.

If *those* treatments don't help you, though, or if they only help you slowly and you start trying things yourself, and those things are associated with cranks and charlatans but also seem to work, well, then, guess what: You've fallen through the floor again, this time through concrete instead of wood, and you're down in whatever is *underneath the basement,* down in the rag-and-bone shop, the deep underground, where the lights are flickering and you're groping with your hands, feeling weird shapes in the half darkness, looking for the ladders but not sure whether they take you back up to normalcy or somewhere else entirely.

What else was down there with me, besides the apparently vast community of Rifers, the Magnetizer with her muscle testing and her chemtrail theories? *The weird shit* was how I described it to myself—the deer on my mother's lawn and the hellmouth beneath its hooves, the dreams with their vampires and armed librarians, the bugs crawling out of the walls of our country house, the sand dollar gleaming ivory beneath my spasm-ridden feet. Was God there? He was supposed to be way up above, enthroned on high, not mucking around in the underground with broken things underfoot and strange machinery half-visible. But maybe His emissaries were down there. Maybe prayers were more effective once you were down there. Maybe it was easier for the signal to reach . . . *somebody* when you weren't inside the bland HGTV living room anymore.

For two and a half years I prayed for help every day, mostly pleading, sometimes bargaining, often stumbling into empty churches the way I did in my long IV summer. The only hints at an answer came in the moments I've already described—the airport encounter with the monk (probably just randomness, I told myself) and the sand dollar on the beach (maybe just a marine creature washed up by coincidence). Then, during the years of excavations, when my immune system seemed to be half working and my various dosages and Rife frequencies had helped me gain some ground, I begged and pleaded less often, and my prayer life lost its hopeless intensity and settled back into the mediocre norm.

At a certain point in this period, I think in the spring of 2018, I went to confession in our parish church in New

Haven—not a terribly frequent occurrence for me in normal times, and even more infrequent during the illness, because the sins I had to confess were mostly just anger and despair, despair and anger, the same depressing round. Coming out of the confessional that day, kneeling to say my ten-Hail-Marys penance in a nearby pew, I realized it had been some time since I'd directed any begging heavenward, and I thought to punctuate the last *Ave* with a plea for help, a self-composed adaptation:

> *Holy Mary, Mother of God,*
> *Intercede for me in your mercy,*
> *That I may be healed of this disease,*
> *Freed of this sickness, and restored to health . . .*

What followed was just as sudden and surprising as the feeling of taking the Tindamax and the antibiotic together, or using the Rife machine for the first time. Once again, it was like being a marionette whose strings were suddenly jerked, my head shaking, my jaw chewing air, my legs kicking, a frantic urge to rub my hands all over my torso. I couldn't stop the feeling, and I couldn't just kneel there, spasming in the pew where anyone might see me. So I staggered out into the vestibule and found a place on the stairs going up to the choir loft, unused and hidden on this weekday, beneath a stained-glass image of the Virgin and the Child. There I half sat and half lay, doing my usual herky-jerky dance, rubbing and panting for the better part of twenty minutes, while a few people filed in for the noon mass without observing me (I hoped). Finally, as the feeling began to leave me, the exhaustion taking over, the daily reading echoed out from the lectern, across the scattering of weekday mass-goers, to reach my still-itching, buzzing ears:

> And the Lord said to Satan, "Have you considered my servant Job, that there is none like him on the earth, a blameless and upright man, who fears God and turns away from evil? He still holds fast his integrity, although you incited me against him to destroy him without reason."
>
> Then Satan answered the Lord and said, "Skin for skin! All that a man has he will give for his life. But stretch out your hand and touch his bone and his flesh, and he will curse you to your face."
>
> And the Lord said to Satan, "Behold, he is in your hand; only spare his life."

I am neither blameless nor upright, but otherwise the timing seemed awfully heavy-handed. And, reader, it made me laugh out loud.

Not for the first time, or the last. In the underneath, there are tears but also laughter, because you know how the things that happen there must seem in the brightly lit normalcy just two stories up. I laughed on the Magnetizer's table, thinking about what my professional world would think of my situation. I laughed when a particular Rife frequency culled from some online testimony did exactly what it was supposed to do, producing exactly the same kind of reaction as an antibiotic dose. I laughed at the experience itself, and also at how decisively it separated me from the simple kind of story, the *normal* kind of story, that I wanted to be able to carry back to the upstairs with me, so that everyone in the HGTV living room could be easily persuaded, so that nobody would look at me like I was a lunatic or dismiss me as a crank. But alas . . .

In the same way, only more so, I laughed when, from that unexpected post-confession Herxheimer onward, at various times and places the experience was reproduced. In the beginning only prayers to Mary seemed to have any effect, but then eventually there were reactions when I asked specific saints for help, beginning with my own namesakes—Gregory (my middle name) and Athanasius, which I had pompously adopted upon conversion—and then others on their feast day or some other moment that suggested them to me. And not only saints: Pushing the boundaries a little further, I sometimes asked for help from departed relatives, on the chance that they had cleared purgatory by now and were in the elevator going up, and in a few cases—a great-grandfather, a grandmother, a relative on Abby's side—it felt like I was answered, with a milder version of the physical shakes, the rubbing and jerking that had pinned me to the church stairs.

Often this answer, this reaction, was mild enough that I could dismiss it as imagination; sometimes I'm sure it *was* just imagination, suggestibility, focusing too closely on the feeling on a given limb. Other times it was bone-shakingly real, and explicable only in three ways. First, as evidence of a mind-body connection in which particular prayers, or just the act of prayer itself, subconsciously flipped a set of switches connecting my brain to my immune system, kicking the latter into a higher gear. Second, as evidence that the whole experience, all the pain and Herxheimers, was just what the skeptical D.C. doctors had assumed: a disturbance in my consciousness that I somehow transferred to my flesh. Or, third, as evidence that down here in the semidarkness, the saints of God were listening, and offering some help.

Whatever the cause, these were not *mystical* encounters, in which the veil was torn and I glad-handed with the angels, or even just felt the self-dissolving oneness with the universe that seems to be the most common kind of numinous experience. In all my years of prayer and churchgoing, I have never had an experience like that. This was entirely embodied and physical, and, like everything else about my long experience of illness, it didn't make my mind or soul feel like something floating free of my body, but quite the reverse. Chronic illness encourages a feeling of mind-body dualism, because you can feel your old self—your true self, or so you think—stuck somewhere inside the body's prison, struggling for survival, waiting for release. But it's a dualism in which the power of the body *over* the mind is made manifest, because the mind is always carapaced by suffering flesh, like a balloon bobbing against a hard ceiling, free to move but not to soar away. And if my prayers were being answered in this case, the only answer was a feeling of further renovation and excavation in the bodily apparatus, which my mind could observe with amused detachment, even laughter, but not somehow escape.

Maybe the answer wasn't about the sickness itself but about how to live with it, because these "extra" experiences began around the time that Abby and I were considering whether I had made enough progress to attempt to have yet one more child—a question that implicated not only my health, her emotional and physical well-being, and our parlous finances, but also the health of the prospective child itself. (I knew, for instance, that spirochetes had been found in the sperm of Lyme-infected men, and that there were childhood cases that looked suspiciously like in utero transmission.) Another child had seemed impossible so long as we still owned the country house, but once it sold and we settled a little more firmly in New Haven, the baby question became *the* question, since it was so time-bound and immediate. We were headed for forty—we couldn't just wait another five years to see if I could shake free of my condition or at least restore our finances to where they'd been before.

No, we had to either leap or not. And the skeptical reader, the psychologically rather than spiritually inclined, is free to read all my attempted communions with saints and ancestors as an attempt to build a permission structure for a possibly foolhardy decision. Indeed, that interpretation and the experience itself aren't so far apart: Wherever the response was coming from, in these prayers I really was probably asking not just for healing but for a kind of permission and support.

The resolution, naturally, had a gothic element. It was a sweltering August, two days before yet another trip to Maine. I woke up in the middle of the night with strong symptoms— an intermittent to rare occurrence now—and descended from our bedroom to sit and commune with the internet for an hour until they abated enough for me to sleep. A few minutes passed, and I became conscious of something brushing at the edges of my consciousness. Not a ghost or angel, but a frantically circling bat.

Somehow I managed to knock it down with blankets, kick it into a cardboard box, and get it out the front door and away into the humid night. But the next day, everyone I told about the incident impressed on me that this had been idiotic, that I should have kept the bat to get it tested for rabies, because it had been flying around for who knows how many hours and there were cases—including a child's death in the 1990s, in a nearby Connecticut town—where a bat had transmitted the disease with a tiny, unnoticed bite.

I would have scoffed at this possibility once, but after my experience with tiny bites and devastating consequences, we figured we should consult some doctors, and, sadly for us, they all ordered us to the emergency room for the first round of rabies shots—a most unwelcome development on what was now the night before we were supposed to drive six hours for vacation.

We were gathering applesauce squeeze packs, to carry our kids through the long ER evening, when my wife decided that, just to be absolutely safe, before we agreed to be jabbed with needles and infused with God knows what, she should probably take a pregnancy test.

And so it was that we first encountered our fourth child, our third daughter—through the telltale pink blur blossoming on a stick as we stood stunned in an upstairs bathroom just before our first all-family ER visit.

Abby did not exactly appreciate it when, once again, I began to laugh.

8

The Island

THERE IS JUST ONE LAST BIT OF CRANKISH, PARANOID business to address before we leave the underneath behind, letting the bats enjoy their caverns undisturbed. That's the question of Lyme disease's origins.

Up in the realm of normalcy, consensus, and responsibly hiked-up socks, there is no real question. We know that *Borrelia* is ancient, that it's long been passed through human hosts, that it was here with the Native Americans, here during the Ice Age. We have a theory—reforestation, suburbanization, the burgeoning deer population—to explain why the disease reemerged so dramatically in the second half of the twentieth century in the American Northeast. We know that it was infecting people in Europe well before Allen Steere gave it a name.

But there is one notable feature of the American Lyme epidemic. If you map its county-by-county incidence, its Northeastern spread forms a kind of semicircle, circumscribed to the east by the Atlantic Ocean, radiating west and north and south from Connecticut and its environs. The darkest zones on this map, close to the center of the imaginary circle, include the Old Lyme area, the eastern end of

Long Island (where it was known as "Montauk knee" because it was common among fishermen), and the nearby islands of Martha's Vineyard and Nantucket (which have the
worst Lyme infection rates in Massachusetts). And right in
the middle of this hot zone is a small island in the Long Island Sound, called Plum Island, which happens to house one
of the U.S. government's biowarfare laboratories.

Like all attractive conspiracy theories, the idea that the
Lyme outbreak somehow started on that island rests on a set
of coincidences. The coincidental location of the laboratory
itself. The coincidence that Willy Burgdorfer, the discoverer
of the spirochete, had connections to the U.S. military bioweapons program, working for years at the U.S. government's Rocky Mountain Laboratories, in Montana, infecting
fleas and mites and ticks with various diseases. The coincidence that the Plum Island laboratory had a tick colony
where similar experiments were conducted. The coincidence that around the same time that Lyme disease emerged
in Connecticut, there were clustered outbreaks of two other
tick-borne illnesses, Rocky Mountain spotted fever and babesiosis, on Nantucket and Martha's Vineyard and Long Island, at a time when neither illness had any East Coast
presence. The coincidence that in the same year when Allen
Steere met Polly Murray and started investigating the strange
outbreak of juvenile arthritis, Plum Island laboratory techs
were experimenting with the Lone Star tick—a so-called
hard tick, which we know is capable of transmitting *Borrelia*.

Even the conspiracy theorists don't think that U.S. scientists in the Cold War era were equipped to use gene editing
to create a new, more virulent *Borrelia* strain. But they con-
ceivably could have developed a more devastating strain
through a kind of forced selection, in which bacteria were

used to infect a large animal population and then harvested from the animals that became particularly ill. Then the escape from Plum Island could have involved the many birds—seagulls, ospreys, Canada geese—that fly back and forth between the island and the inhabited coastlines north and south. A tick would have fed on an infected animal in one of the island's outdoor pens (if you imagine a U.S. bioweapons laboratory as a perfectly antiseptic facility, think again), picked up the new strain, and then crawled over to where a seabird was picking a morsel from the animals' feeding trough (something that Plum Island workers allegedly witnessed happening) and hitched a ride on the bird back to the mainland.

Notably, nothing about this requires a malevolent government plot to infect the Eastern Seaboard. It just requires a certain negligence about safety protocols, amply documented in Michael Christopher Carroll's history of Plum Island, *Lab 257*, and the larger folly of building a bioweapons facility on a major bird migration route.

At the same time, like all conspiracy theories that remain, well, just that, the Lyme–Plum Island connection is a circumstantial narrative in search of a smoking gun. The theorists offer a shifting range of possibilities for when they think the escape happened: Maybe the disease broke out in the 1970s, spread by the Lone Star tick (Carroll argues that security in the laboratory decayed after the 1950s); maybe it first broke out in the 1940s, when the Plum Island biowarfare experiments began (which would explain why the Murray family fell sick in the 1960s). They have no definitive evidence that the laboratory ever experimented specifically with the *Borrelia* spirochete or deer ticks. And while their theory is compatible with genetic evidence for *Borrelia's* antiquity in North America—since they aren't arguing that the experiments invented the spirochete, just that they somehow made it more devastating—their focus on the suspicious map of the Northeastern outbreak doesn't explain the parallel, but geographically separate, growth of Lyme infections in Wisconsin, Minnesota, and California over the last few decades. That spread, Midwestern and West Coast, tracks with the gradual post-1960s expansion of tick habitats in both regions—fitting with the suburban-reemergence theory, with no need for any kind of biowarfare trigger.

So even with all those piled-up coincidences around Plum Island, a revival of an old disease under the peculiar ecological pressure of suburban growth still seems like the most parsimonious explanation for the Lyme epidemic. And for the old me, the unsickened and reasonable self of 2015, that parsimony would be enough.

The new me, though, looks at the circumstantial evidence through eyes that are more disillusioned with official narratives, more willing to consider the theory even if I don't quite believe.

At the very least, there is one definite revelation contained in all the Plum Island speculation: Whether or not Lyme disease is actually some kind of bioweapon, the idea of unleashing a Lyme-like sickness on unsuspecting human populations was a real part of American military thinking in the Cold War.

This was not at all how I imagined bioweapons programs. Perhaps thanks to one too many readings of *The Stand* as an impressionable kid, I assumed that they mostly proceeded along a go-big-or-go-home, mass-fatalities-or-nothing vector, looking for the next plague and superflu, or at least a

COVID-19-level killer. *What kind of bioweapons program would work with ticks and tick-borne illness?* I remember thinking when someone first shared the Plum Island scenario with me. *You're going to lay an enemy society low with crawling bugs and chronic sickness? Really?*

But then I read *Bitten: The Secret History of Lyme Disease and Biological Weapons,* a recent book by Kris Newby, a Lyme-afflicted writer and documentarian. In one sense, the book illustrates the limits of the Plum Island theories, the way they keep falling short of proof. It exists because Willy Burgdorfer, in interviews in his last years, made a lot of strange comments about Lyme disease, seeming to hint that the pathogen he helped discover might have been connected to the same bioweapons programs that he had once assisted. But Burgdorfer was suffering from Parkinson's at the time of these interviews, and he passed away without supplying clarity. Newby tries to put the fragmentary comments together with suspicious details from Burgdorfer's Lyme investigations in the 1980s, when she thinks that his old friends in the military persuaded him to drop the line of investigation pointing to an accidental biolab release. But her own investigations repeatedly dead-end, and her theories feel more like speculative exercises than explanations for everything weird about the Lyme epidemic.

What's more striking in Newby's book is the publicly available backstory, the strange history of military experiments with ticks and infectious agents, which answers my incredulous question: *Chronic illness as biowarfare? Really?* Something along those lines was, in fact, the military's thinking. "The advantages of arthropods as BW [bioweapon] carriers" were taken seriously by America's Cold War–era military command, Newby reports, and while the optimal bioweapon would be a fatal virus (one of Burgdorfer's projects tried to infect mosquitoes with a particularly deadly version of yellow fever), there was plenty of research work on merely incapacitating conditions, and strategic planning that envisioned their use in theaters from Korea to the Caribbean.

For instance, in a situation like the thirty-eighth-parallel stalemate on the Korean Peninsula, military planners contemplated the mass release of infected ticks as a kind of biological minefield, "keeping an area constantly dangerous" in a way that other bioweapons might not. In other contexts, Newby notes that the military considered scenarios where a bioweapon might make "a large percentage of a population moderately ill for weeks to months" with something "hard to diagnose and treat." The obvious application was to Castro's Cuba, the target of so many American military schemes in the 1960s, including one that involved using a biological agent to put workers in the cane fields and sugar mills "out of action . . . for the remainder of this harvest." Such a planned outbreak could be a form of economic sabotage, or it could be a prelude to a military offensive, making it "easier for invading, vaccinated soldiers to take over" without the sickened population putting up a fight.

So, as strange as it seems, a scenario where some American enemy—Korean or Cuban, Russian or Red Chinese—could be dosed en masse with something like my own tick-borne infection was not only pondered but actively pursued by the United States government in the early Cold War years. (Though one assumes the frigid Russian winter would be as hard on ticks as it was on Napoleon and Hitler.) And despite finding the idea absurd at first, I have come around to the strategic plausibility of this approach: A nation full of people in the shape that I was in during my first year of illness would, indeed, be a nation ripe for conquest, confused and despairing and ready to succumb.

It's a peculiar thought, this, especially given how often I thought in martial metaphors during my treatment. Whether or not some slipshod procedure on an island in the Long Island Sound directly contributed to my infection, the *idea* of deliberately giving my sickness, in all its frustrating and devastating particulars, to as many people as possible was probably pondered by men in military uniforms and lab coats—as something one might regrettably need to do to others, to potentially millions of others, for the sake of a speedy victory in a necessary war.

I SAW THE ISLAND ONCE. IT WAS IN THE SUMMER AFTER WE landed in New Haven, when my mother-in-law rented a house on the North Fork of Long Island and we spent a week there with our kids and several of my in-laws. The house had a smooth green lawn spread out on a high plateau above the beach, and the grass was absolutely crawling with deer ticks, more than we ever saw in the meadows and grass around our haunted country house. Several of them were latched on to our kids; one had dug a little ways into our younger daughter's belly. ("Mommy, I think my mole is moving," she moaned in the bathroom.) She and my sister-in-law both had to get a prophylactic antibiotic dose.

For the trip back, we took the ferry from Orient Point to New London, and as we churned across the Sound I realized that we'd be passing very close to Plum Island. It was a fogbound afternoon, and I had just climbed to the cool mists of the upper deck, a light pain pulsing in my ears, when the island loomed up suddenly to port. There were deep woods all along the shore and then, around a natural harbor, a sprawl of white buildings. I knew that parts of the facility were still open, but this looked like some derelict settlement or lost colony, part Roanoke and part Jurassic Park.

For a long moment I stared at the ghostly buildings, the distance narrowing and widening. Then the fog eddied around the shore and swallowed them, swallowed everything the way I gulped a handful of pills—woods and rocky shore as well as buildings—while a gull screamed and the ferry's wake boiled, the big boat carrying us northward and away.

I watched for another moment, still looking for shapes in the mist, and then I turned and took my pain below.

9

Pandemia

IF I WAS WELL ENOUGH FOR US TO HAVE ONE MORE CHILD, then I was well enough to write about the whole experience. That was what I told myself in late 2019, after years of silent swearing that I wouldn't write about my illness—not a single word, despite all the words my job required—until I could declare victory, describe the illness in the past tense, and boast that I knew how to get rid of chronic Lyme disease because I had gotten rid of it myself.

It was a solid plan in theory, but by now I had been sick for almost half a decade, and while I believed in my continuing progress, Zeno's paradox still haunted me: If I waited for full health, for a daily life without any trace of pain, I might be waiting another five or ten years, with slower and slower increments of progress the further on I went. Meanwhile, I had managed two other long writing projects during more difficult phases of the illness, and this one suddenly acquired the feeling of compulsion, like a place I had to scratch or rub: I wrote the initial sketch for this book's opening chapters in just three days, which seemed like a sign that the story was ready to be told.

It helped that after our family survived the rabies shots

(which gave me their own set of strange sensations, needless to say) and entered fully into the fall and winter of Abby's fourth pregnancy, I seemed to have reached a new and better equilibrium. My symptoms could be mild, even spectral, for many days at a time. I could go off antibiotics for weeklong stretches without having to rush upstairs to the Rife machine every few hours. The main problem was the run of colds that my kids kept bringing home from school, which were still guaranteed to bring the old pain rushing back in earnest. But if I could just avoid having any *other* viruses or bacteria penetrate my body, I could pass weeks without losing more than an hour at a time to back or head or chest pain, without having the full-day meltdowns that had long been a reliable part of even my partially recovered life.

For New Year's Eve, the turn from 2019 to 2020, we visited my wife's best friend and her family in Minnesota. It was the second time we had made the trip since I fell sick, and the contrast was instructive. On the previous journey, over two years earlier, I had been in pain more or less constantly, with maybe an hour's break here or there. That trip had included a professional excursion to a nearby college, where I had participated in an event with Cornel West—a very successful evening mostly because of his charisma and good cheer, but one in which I was called upon to practice my own kind of bonhomie, which was entirely at odds with how my body felt.

Afterward I pulled over on a windswept north country highway to get gas. As the rented minivan's tank filled up I stood in the cold, stuffing down a Snickers bar and rubbing at my neck, thinking about what it means to be a sick but functional person, capable of fulfilling obligations but unable to find enjoyment in between. *You have to live for others,* I told myself (*crunch* went the Snickers), thinking about the entertained college audience; about our daughters, who were having a great time with our hosts' kids; about Abby, who was always happier around her friend . . . and I tried to draw something for myself out from their happiness, some sense of accomplishment to make my own life of pain and purpose feel not just bearable, a candy-bar-punctuated endurance test, but actually worthwhile.

But the second Minnesota visit, two years later, was much better. Now the hours spent in pain were the exceptional ones, and I could run through a meal, a movie, even most of a Mall of America trek without thinking more than occasionally about my body and its problems. In my world of increments and endless peelings, of tiny gains from week to week or month to month, this over-the-years perspective was the only way to see that, yes, for certain, I was achieving something. If I could come this far, I could hope to come all the way, to cross the frontier and leave the country of suffering behind.

On New Year's Eve I walked out along the winding driveway that led from our friends' house back to their exurban road. The previous day, there had been a Minnesota dusting of snow—a blizzard by our Eastern standards—and the moon and stars were bright above the bare white landscape. It was a good landscape for reflection. The year was turning: I had a new book coming out, I was plotting this one, Abby was at work on a new book too, we were having another baby, we were starting to save a little money once again, and, however slowly, I was, by the grace of God, getting better.

2020, I told myself, *is going to be a good year.*

. . .

I REALIZED THAT IT WOULDN'T BE GOOD SOONER THAN MOST people. In the weeks from late January to late February, when the seriousness of the coronavirus threat hadn't yet become a partisan issue and the mood among mainstream experts was sanguine, I was staring at grainy videos from Wuhan and reading dire predictions from right-wing eccentrics. If I had learned anything from almost five years of illness, it was to trust my own read on a situation at least as much I trusted reassurances from the medical establishment. So I gave up handshaking before anybody else I knew; I was the only non-Asian mask wearer on a cross-country flight; I filled our cellar with toilet paper and canned goods weeks before the shortages began; I stockpiled masks when we were still being told they didn't work.

But my mix of paranoia and self-confidence was its own form of hubris. My new book was coming out, I needed to go on tour to sell it, to make the most of the opportunity to rebuild our finances, to push my semi-recovered body as far as it could be pushed . . . and so I told myself that I could travel safely if I took enough precautions, and then cut short my trips before community spread began in earnest. Having been ahead of the experts, I thought I could stay ahead of the virus itself.

My projections weren't completely wrong, but for all my distrust of experts, I still overestimated the competence of the CDC and the FDA in tracking and testing for the virus, and I underestimated how far the disease could spread without our being generally aware that it was present. So I returned from the last leg of my truncated book tour the day before Connecticut closed its schools, congratulated myself on my good timing . . . and the next morning woke up to a sore throat, a dry cough, and pain of a very different sort than I was used to, spreading in my lungs.

This time I wasn't ill alone. Once more I went to the ER, where no tests were yet available, so I was advised to go home and self-quarantine—but too late. Within a day it was clear that I had managed to pass along the infection to Abby, now seven months pregnant, our kids, my mother, and (I suspect, though her case was very mild) my mother-in-law as well. My son had it the worst of our kids, with a terrible racking chest cough for many days and (for us, sleepless) nights. My own case was the most conventional: first the cough and the lung pain and then a frightening shortness of breath—an interesting novelty after so many years of the same cycling of symptoms, but not one to be greeted with delight.

It was a week before I managed to get tests, for my son and myself only. Ten days later we were informed that his test had been botched and therefore was inconclusive, while mine was negative.

A past version of myself might have been tempted to believe the result. The new version, the one accustomed to inconclusive tests and self-doctoring, considered my distinctive symptoms (despite innumerable colds, I had never been short of breath in forty years of life), plus my family's distinctive symptoms (my son had never been this sick before, my wife's lungs had never felt so strange), plus the timing and my New York–D.C.–L.A. travel, plus the fact that the tests at that point had at least a 40 percent false-negative rate, and felt entirely comfortable with self-diagnosis: The test was wrong, and we definitely had the virus.

And this new version of myself also immediately leaped

into action to do something about it, even though, of course, officially there was nothing to be done—dosing myself with immune-system boosters, acquiring allegedly antiviral herbs, poring through the Rife book for frequencies that seemed like they might be a good fit. (There was no COVID-19 channel, obviously, but there were several suggestions for "coronaviruses" and a few for "RNA virus infections.") And long before it was picked up by Donald Trump, back when it was just an internet theory based on French and Chinese trials, I knew all about hydroxychloroquine—which had been prescribed to me by the Reassurer long ago, in a bottle that still had a few pills remaining, which I now found and took.

Was this behavior mad or sensible? There were too many variables to know for sure. Demographically, I was a relatively low-risk COVID case, though slightly higher-risk for being male. On the other hand, at this point—mid-March of 2020—we still knew precious little about its real fatality rate and long-term consequences, and I was intimately familiar with just how *long-term* an illness's consequences could be. There was also no way to know how it would interact with my residual, un-excavated Lyme, which predictably flared up along with the novel illness. I felt pretty terrible in an unusually frightening way, the breathing problems inspiring fears I hadn't felt since my phantom heart attacks five years before—so whatever version of the virus I had, it definitely wasn't the "mild" or "asymptomatic" variety.

And all my biases now were against patience and trust, and in favor of swift experimentation. So experiment is what I did.

. . .

MY OWN CASE TO ONE SIDE, THE CORONAVIRUS ERA SOON came to feel like a shattered mirror of the tick-borne epidemic and its controversies, with different pieces of the Lyme wars reflected and refracted in different aspects of the worldwide COVID crisis. Things that came as a surprise to people for whom modern medicine was still a stable floor—the testing that didn't work, the confident medical advice that had to be reversed and then reversed again, the wild uncertainty about how, and for how long, a single pathogen's symptomatic effects might manifest themselves—were completely unsurprising to me by now. The debate over COVID's origins, both the connection to animals and the lab-leak hypothesis—first dismissed as paranoia, then more seriously considered—were equally familiar, with the Wuhan Institute of Virology occupying the same suspicious position near the COVID epicenter as Plum Island occupied in the Lyme epidemic. Even our rural fantasy, the precipitating factor in my sickness, made a strange reappearance, with countless professionals suddenly following *their* rural fantasies in hopes of escaping the airborne virus's reach, all unaware that a very different, slower-working enemy awaited in the high fields, the tumbled stone walls.

Meanwhile, the positions of the warring Lyme camps were echoed in various ways by the different factions in the COVID wars. For instance, what soon became the most outsiderish, anti-establishment position, taken up by much of the Trumpist and libertarian right as a cudgel against the lockdowns and the liberals who supported them—that the disease was *just the flu,* that the sick were exaggerating their symptoms and the doctors treating them were overdiagnosing the disease—contained within it attitudes and impulses that Lyme patients encounter from within the medical establishment all the time. That meant that in the COVID era I found myself having Twitter arguments with contrarian and crankish outsiders, urging them to take the disease more seriously, that resembled my past disagreements with consummate medical insiders over their underdiagnosis and dismissiveness toward Lyme.

So I was finally on the side of the medical establishment, in one sense. But at the same time, the establishment was obviously freaked out by the proliferation of non-approved, non-expert speculation about the illness on the internet, and the Lyme experience made me a lot more sympathetic to this kind of speculation. Some nodes in the online hive mind specialized in dumb, COVID-skeptical takes, but others were way out ahead of the World Health Organization and other expert entities when it came to the benefits of mask wearing or the low likelihood of surface transmission. Some generated bogus proofs for speculative treatments, but others focused on below-the-radar variables—vitamin D exposure, for instance—that may still prove to make a difference. And in other cases there was just a gray area, where neither the experts nor the internet knew what really worked. Everyone was groping and arguing in the basement beneath the certain floor of knowledge, if not the way-down-underneath.

The hydroxychloroquine debate was a good example. The initial support for the drug came from anecdata, from doctors using it in Asia and then Europe and reporting good results for patients who took it early in the course of the disease. Then it was taken up by a shaggy-haired French doctor, Didier Raoult, who resembled many Lyme specialists I'd met: eccentric and self-confident and brilliant, easy to dismiss as a crank but also the sort of person who might champion a helpful treatment early. Then Trump started touting the drug as some sort of miracle cure, and you could see the establishment narrative harden, cyst-like, in response—this was an "unproven" and "dubious" treatment with dangerous side effects (even though two billion people had taken it at some point in their lives), and anyone who experimented with it as a COVID-19 treatment was simply reckless (never mind that the alternative for high-risk patients who got the virus at that point was to try . . . nothing). And then came the big, definitive *Lancet* study showing that not only was the drug ineffective, but 30 percent more COVID patients died when they took it as compared with a placebo.

Case closed—except *then* came the retraction of the big study, which turned out to be, in the words of *The Lancet*'s editor, a "fabrication" and "a monumental fraud." A study from Detroit's Henry Ford Hospital followed, showing success using the drug for early cases. But it wasn't a randomized controlled trial; the media treated it critically, and even more so when Trump allies touted it. Another study came out, this time with a randomized design, showing poor effects for the drug. This one got more favorable press attention, but the study had concentrated the drug's use among the sickest patients, which wasn't the initial claim for how and when it worked. And so it went, a ping-pong of studies, a polarized response, and a palpable desire in the health bureaucracy to "move on" to less controversial treatments.

In just a few months, then, an obscure malaria drug had managed to generate the kind of divisions that Lyme disease had taken years and years to forge, with conflicts between widespread anecdote, on the one hand, and the demand for certainty and rigor, on the other—between an experimental approach to medicine and a bureaucratic disapproval of unproven treatments, all of it heightened by the pandemic's stakes and Trump-era polarization.

It was a case study in a larger pandemic-era theme: the gulf between the confidence in institutions that the media, especially, wanted to shore up, and the much messier reality. *Trust the science,* people said throughout, often as an understandable response to Trump's constant stream of bullshit, but the slogan kept running aground on the reality that official science is filtered through fallible institutions, politicized processes, and bureaucratic incentives, which throughout the crisis were amply on display.

You couldn't trust the CDC to roll out a reliable coronavirus test: They botched it, and a lab in Washington State had to fill the breach. You couldn't trust the FDA to be creative in the face of thousands of Americans dying every day: Operation Warp Speed delivered vaccines astonishingly quickly, but the FDA stuck with a cautious approval process, even for vaccines that were already approved in Europe and South Korea. You couldn't trust the WHO to even acknowledge that the virus was primarily airborne, until months and months after everyone who followed the data took for granted that it was. And from the beginning of the pandemic to its still-unfinished end, there were weirdos on the internet who were more reliable guides to what was happening, what was possible, and what should actually be done than Anthony Fauci or any other official information source.

If you take all these COVID-era tendencies and imagine them applied to a debate over a more shadowy disease, one that incapacitates but rarely kills, whose spread has happened slowly, without blaring headlines and immense political pressure to *do something* in response—well, then you've imagined the flawed medical system, the institutional science, that has helped the Lyme epidemic keep burning to this day.

THE MOST DIRECT PARALLEL BETWEEN THE LYME EXPERIence and the coronavirus drama, though, was in the swift proliferation of chronic cases from the new disease. These were the people, usually younger than the fatal cases, who got sick and didn't die but didn't seem to get better, either. They spent months bedridden and exhausted, they ran fevers that didn't break, they reported effects from the sickness not just in their throat or lungs but all over, in the heart and kidneys, joints and muscles, bowels and brain.

After months of illness, a female colleague, younger than me and doubtless healthier, still couldn't walk more than two blocks without pausing, short of breath. One of my college roommates who lived in Queens was sick for three weeks in March and seemed to quickly recover, only to find himself plagued by recurring chest pain, more in the heart than in the lungs, which sent him—like me, five years earlier—to emergency rooms and cardiologists with no result. When a New Yorker named Hannah Davis passed her four-month mark after infection, in late July of 2020, she tweeted a list of symptoms that reminded me of the letters that desperate Lyme patients sent to Allen Steere in the 1990s, begging to be taken seriously:

> I still have a near-daily fever, loss of cognitive function, essential tremors, GI issues, severe headaches, heartrate of 150+, viral arthritis, heart palpitations, muscle aches, a feeling like my body has forgotten to breathe. Over the past 124 days I've lost all feeling in my arms & hands, had ex-

treme back/kidney/rib pain, phantom smells (like someone BBQing bad meat), tinnitus, difficulty understanding
text/reading, difficulty following conversations, sensitivity
to noise & light, nonstop bruising. ★Thinking★ can cause
headaches now.

Nobody knew exactly what to do for these "long haul"
COVID patients, and, as with Lyme patients there were
plenty of stories about sufferers being dismissed and disbe-
lieved, especially in cases where they had tested negative or
(often, in those days) simply been unable to get a test to
confirm their diagnosis.

At the same time, though, the scope and speed of
COVID's airborne spread, the fact that there were so many
of these long-haul patients all at once, seemed to create more
sympathy and straightforward belief for their stories than
in the slower-building tick-borne epidemic. So, perhaps, did
the fact that doctors and nurses were disproportionately represented among early COVID cases, and thus among long-
haulers, too.

In October of 2020, *The Wall Street Journal* covered some
of these doctors, many of them months into a twilight existence of chronic fatigue and heart palpitations and headaches. One of them, just two years removed from running
the New York City Marathon, described going to a pulmo-
nologist for her racing heartbeat and being told to try psy-
chiatry and Xanax: "I said, 'I don't think so, I'm a psychiatrist.'"
Another, an emergency physician in Atlanta, told the *Journal*
that "this has absolutely changed my perspective . . . [on] the
patients I see who come in with symptoms that are very real
and I can't find any objective data to point me to a certain
diagnosis."

So COVID offered a terrible crash-course education in the reality of chronic illness, the gap between what a disease was supposed to do in its "normal" presentation (symptoms in the throat and lungs for the coronavirus, a bull's-eye rash and fever and joint pain for Lyme) and how often the actual presentation is something else entirely, how many weird cascades a single invader can set off, how easily a previously healthy person can fall into a pit.

Who knows whether this education will change the way chronic illnesses are treated in the long run. Much of the medical theorizing about long-haul COVID, so far, has followed tracks familiar to Lyme patients—treating the recurring symptoms as problems of inflammation and tissue damage, a disturbed autonomic nervous system or an autoimmune cascade, which need to be managed palliatively or suppressed while the body is trained back to health through exercise or just recovers on its own. For patients who don't seem to make much progress, there are grim comparisons to chronic fatigue syndrome, fibromyalgia, and, yes, "post-treatment" Lyme—but as with official discussions of those conditions, the possibility that a pathogen lingers is downplayed, and the assumption is that most of the suffering are fully in the aftermath of their infection.

Patience may well be the right approach for a lot of long-haul cases, who do seem to improve just by gradually building up their strength, slowly extending themselves in exercise as their hearts and lungs get back to normal. My colleague's case has been like that, and maybe my mother's as well: She feels okay six months after falling ill but gets chest pain and exhaustion when she does too much yard work.

On the other hand, people like Hannah Davis who have symptoms that seem to pop up randomly around the body, with kidney pain one day and neuropathies the next and brain fog all the while—it seems an awful lot like the way Lyme and other tick-borne travelers persist inside afflicted flesh, their effects cropping up all over long after the acute initial phase is done. A virus is not a burrowing spirochete, but we know that viral infections, too, can persist and re-appear. In the case of chronic fatigue syndrome, for instance, some doctors believe that the Epstein-Barr virus, often the triggering pathogen, sticks around to cause the ongoing immune disturbances, much as COVID-19 might in long-haul patients.

So to hear the term "post-COVID syndrome" already being tossed around to describe people whose COVID experience feels continuous, just months and months of the same feelings the virus gave them from the start—well, let's just say it sounds unfortunately familiar, and not necessarily a good sign for bringing them fully back to health.

I WAS TECHNICALLY A COVID LONG-HAULER, BY THE OF-ficial standard of symptoms that last beyond an initial month. Unlike my mother, with her stressed-out chest muscles, and Abby, with her scorched-feeling lungs, my persisting symptoms were a little more acute. My breathing difficulties mostly went away after I took the hydroxychloroquine (quite possibly a coincidence, of course), and three weeks after the initial cough I thought I had recovered. But then, like clockwork, every week or two thereafter, I would have a day or more of strange internal pain, sometimes in my lungs, sometimes in my guts, sometimes down in my lower back in what I assume was my kidneys. This was an interesting experience (he said, with clinical detachment), because it was similar to my years of Lyme pain in its migratory and temporary qualities, but completely different in other ways: It felt much more like my organs hurt, not my joints or muscles, and nothing that I did or tried to take for it produced anything like the Herxheimer effect.

The one thing that did seem to shorten the periods of pain belonged, naturally, to my rag-and-bone-shop treatments: It was a twenty-eight-minute audio file, produced by some kind of sound-healing, New Age outfit called FRQNCY, that when I googled "COVID Rife" showed up on Spotify under the title "Anti-Coronavirus/COVID-19 Frequency." When I listened to it during bouts of pain, there was a quickening and then a faster abatement.

Just another totally normal and reasonable experience, nothing strange about it.

Overall abatement took about five months: The recurrences stretched further and further apart after May, and the last time I felt the organ pain was late August of 2020, six months ago as I write these words. So I am telling myself, however presumptuously, that this was one chronic illness that my body could actually beat.

My original illness, meanwhile, emerged from my coronavirus infection still intact but changed. During the acute phase, it was amplified: In the days when my lungs were most affected by COVID, I was getting waves of joint and muscle pain, in both the Lyme and *Bartonella* spots, that were stronger than anything I'd felt in at least a year. But then the tick-borne symptoms diminished, and for a while in that strange summer I imagined writing an improbable ending to this story in which it took one pandemic to cure another—in which my body's immune response to the coronavirus was finally enough to rout the tick-borne invaders too.

As with other hopeful endings I pitched to myself, that isn't quite what happened. But it did feel like some larger-than-usual layer had been removed during the pandemic spring and summer, and what remained—what remains now, as I write—was buried extremely deep, not in my knee but deep inside the kneecap, not in my eyes but way back in the socket, not in my balls but up against the pubic bone, not just in my chest and throat but way down deep, where the esophagus meets the stomach.

I was no longer rubbing and itching and gyrating when I treated these symptoms from my apothecary's chest. Instead I tensed and flexed, I squeezed and stretched, and sometimes I even *tapped* on bones and joints—like a miner with a pickax, testing for a seam or looking for some hollow space far down beneath the earth.

AND THERE WAS CHANGE OF ANOTHER KIND, OF COURSE: Our fourth child and third daughter was born in late April of that year, seven weeks after I came home sick, in a hospital like a ghost town, on the very day the pandemic's spring death rate peaked in our home state.

We brought her home, healthy and fat-cheeked and as cheerful as any of her siblings, apparently untouched by COVID, Lyme, or rabies. And she sprawls beside me now, toying with the fringes of a blanket, her mere existence a rebuke to all our doubts about conceiving her, and her life a vindication of everything I've done to try to save my own.

10

The Permeable Body

THE PHILOSOPHER CHARLES TAYLOR ONCE DESCRIBED the life of the modern world in terms of a striking metamorphosis. The change that came in with the Renaissance and the Scientific Revolution, he argued, wasn't so much a change of belief as a change in how the human self related to the universe. It wasn't just that in the past people were more likely to believe in the existence of devils or angels or spirits. They also believed that their own selves were permeable, vulnerable to external influence from the supernatural realm. Their world "was one in which these forces could cross a porous boundary and shape our lives, psychic and physical," where spiritual influence could be exerted from a distance and invasion and possession were perils that every human being faced.

Moderns, on the other hand, see ourselves as "buffered"—with a strong sense of our own boundaries, of the difference between the world *out there* and the person *in here,* and relatively little reason to worry about the kind of invasive experience that a more enchanted worldview took for granted. Where "the porous self is vulnerable: to spirits, demons, cosmic forces . . . the buffered self has been taken out of the world of this kind of fear."

The successes of modern medicine have extended this transformation to the way that we think about our bodies and contagion. The old idea that people fell ill from bad airs and bodily humors made illness seem miasmic, omnipresent, inescapably part of what the body breathed and pumped and circulated. The germ theory of disease, on the other hand, allowed for a stricter separation between the body and external perils, with disease something entirely separate, a distinct life-form that, with enough buffering, could be excluded from the secure, protected flesh. Then the combination of vaccination and antibiotics built the walls and policed the borders. Not completely, of course: The common cold and healthy gut bacteria remained to remind us of our permeability. But the change still enabled human beings to experience illness more as an external threat to a well-protected body and less as something inescapable that could enter easily and set up camp beneath their skin.

The coronavirus has been one kind of challenge to this dispensation—the first novel disease in my lifetime that moved through air and breath and found our systems wide open and undefended to its often fatal touch. But chronic illness is another kind of challenge, because it suggests an inherent porousness and vulnerability, where something can get in unnoticed, evade tests and drugs alike, and linger and spread for years, forging a kind of painful symbiosis with the body.

Based on my own experience, at least, many doctors seem almost offended by the kind of permeability that the chronic-illness experience implies. It's easier for them to believe that something has simply gone wrong internally, the machine breaking down or running the wrong program, because in that case the body's buffered status is preserved. It's even easier for them to fall back on a mind-body mysterianism, to blame pain and suffering on something they can't observe or measure, than to allow that things might *get in* despite a negative test and *stay in* despite a round of antibiotics. That possibility seems to call into question one of the primary achievements of their guild: the protection of the body from dangers, its armoring against a hostile world.

I don't come to bury this achievement. For the past six years I have relied on modern medicine to fight my disease, and my goal has always been to restore a version of what the modern vision promises—my tissue and bloodstream purged of tick-borne bacteria, my body's invader or enemy expelled, my body's hatches securely battened down again.

There may be other ways to be healed of a chronic affliction, ways to achieve balance between your body and the things that slip inside without just killing them in large numbers, but I haven't found them. For me it has always been a war, and I have come back toward health by fighting for every inch of territory.

But throughout that fight I have also gained a heightened awareness that the territory really is an ecosystem, an actual terrain, with different viral and bacterial forces moving through the landscape temporarily, various influences being exerted from outside—magnets, sound waves, maybe even the prayers of holy saints—and hidden places everywhere that are hospitable to many kinds of life. The body isn't a clean machine that sometimes breaks or leaks or rusts. It's a landscape in which many things take root. At the worst of my sickness, I sometimes had an image of a corpse in the deep woods, fertilizing the plants that grow in and around and through it, feeding the insects that swarm over it, surrounding the tree roots that grow through its rib cage as its flesh decays into the earth. *Remember thou art dust,* runs the Christian admonition, *and to dust you shall return.* But dust is dead, while the earth to which we return is very much alive. So it might be amended: Remember that your body comes out of nature, and nature can always possess it once again.

The feeling of possession by another life-form, by spirochetes or parasites or viruses, isn't the same as the supernatural possession that was so much more feared in the past. A bacterium won't speak with your voice in ancient languages or induce you to levitate above a baffled priest. But neither are the two entirely distinct. An invading illness doesn't have the malign intelligence ascribed to devils, but it can still use you for its evolutionary end. My own mind felt constantly besieged during the worst of my sickness, and there were fleeting moments when it seemed as though the invasion had literally displaced my normal consciousness, installing something despairing or rageful in its place. And other sufferers I've met, for whom brain fog and other mental symptoms were much worse, report a different kind of displacement amid a Lyme infection, where the mind or self is shoved aside and a kind of *nothing* takes its place, something without memory or purpose, like the literal expression of a mindless bacterium, not possession but dispossession, with a nullity where the self should rightfully be.

The ragefulness I felt and still occasionally feel, the urge to rant and curse, is also reportedly a common feeling. And this rage means more, for some sufferers, than just the simmering anger that the chronically ill might reasonably feel toward the medical system or their situation—something more overwhelming, more inhuman and antihuman, more (let's just say it) demoniacal. Again, this is not the same as actual possession, but neither is it worlds apart: You don't need to have a literal demon in your head to feel a devilish contempt for life, an omnidirectional hatred, a desire to blaspheme against anything and everything—your loving family, your own mind and body, God Himself. Including a God you don't believe exists.

Part of this aspect of chronic illness is captured in the critically garlanded off-Broadway play *Heroes of the Fourth Turning,* about a collection of friends from a small conservative Catholic college gathering years after their graduation to reckon with the disappointing turns their lives have taken since—one's failure to launch, another's morally compromised career in right-wing politics, and so on. The character who seems the kindest and most Christian of the four, a young woman named Emily, is suffering from an unnamed illness that has her hobbling everywhere in terrific pain. The playwright's sister suffered for years from chronic Lyme disease, and we are invited to assume that Emily has the same affliction.

At some point one of her friends is waxing philosophical about the problems of gnosticism, the denial that the body is actually connected to the soul, and she says, "Oh that's beautiful J, that's so—my body is so much a part of me I can't even begin . . . And I didn't choose this, my body is just a friggin prairie of pain, and I can't choose to make it go away."

The prairie of pain, the suffering body as the suffering landscape, is the best description of the pain of Lyme I've heard or read. But the stronger shock of recognition comes at the end of the play, when, amid an increasingly apocalyptic mood, Emily suddenly vomits up a monologue, a scream of world-rejecting fury.

The play's interpreters are still arguing over what the scene means—whether she's suffering vicariously for all her struggling friends or whether she herself is possessed by the same demon hanging out behind the house. But to watch Emily's monologue while sharing in her illness is to recognize the scene on a much more basic level: Whatever its substantive meaning, it's a faithful transcription of a mood, a spirit, an overspilling mix of fury and exhaustion and despair, that everyone afflicted with a chronic infection can recognize. Not possession in the classic sense, but still a sense that something is inside you that wants your destruction, that sets fire to the fields of your flesh, that mindlessly partakes in the unsleeping mind of hell.

THAT'S THE DARKEST PLACE; NOW LET'S HAVE SOME LIGHT. Because the other thing that an invasive chronic illness shares with the experience of spiritual possession is that it is not necessarily permanent. Just as the possessed person experiences a taste of hell but isn't actually damned, the body inhabited by sickness has something in common with the corpse in the forest, the rotting flesh and mossy bone, but with the crucial difference that the sickened body isn't finished yet.

This isn't always experienced as a gift. *Lyme doesn't kill you,* runs one of the mordant mottoes of the chronic-Lyme community, *it just makes you wish that you were dead.* I certainly wished that from time to time; I know that others with the disease, more besieged or overwhelmed by neurological symptoms, wish it more often, even to self-harm or suicide attempts.

But in my years of fighting for my own life, I've also watched diseases that don't give their victims the opportunity to fight back, the time to find the right doctor or the right regimen, the chance to experiment with the weirdest medicines and discover one that works.

Two of the best people I knew were claimed by cancer in these years, both, like us, parents of young children, both of them better Christians than I could ever claim to be. The first was a close friend of Abby's, who was diagnosed with colon cancer in the same year that I fell sick, and who had finished a first, successful-seeming round of treatment when I was sinking to my nadir. I remember going to a pool in the D.C. suburbs with her and her husband and her daughter in the first summer of my sickness, when we were both gaunt and strange, but she was optimistic, on the rebound, and I was lost in my dark wood. I was still lost a year later when her cancer came back and the treatments failed, and we drove down from our miserable exile in Connecticut to the Maryland hospice where she lay dying. There was grace there, a sense that she seemed to have already partially passed over, that she was looking at us, at our struggles, with an almost supernatural sympathy. But her suffering body, the desolation of her husband, the child she left behind—it was simply a different order of experience from what we were going through, and the only message to us as spectators, whether or not I could receive it, was that we were fortunate, so fortunate, to have a different cup to drink than theirs.

In 2020 that cup was given to a New Haven friend of mine named Andrew, a Knight of Columbus and energetic global diplomat who was saving Middle Eastern Christians from the Islamic State while I was wandering our rural property and dosing myself with tetracycline and tweeting against Trump. He and his wife had their fourth child just a couple of months before we had ours, and then it happened: a leukemia diagnosis in the midst of the pandemic. A round of intense treatment seemed to go well and had him back home by early fall, but then in October the cancer returned, too fast for any help. He died on the evening before the Feast of All Saints, the same day that the Knights' founder, the New Haven priest Michael J. McGivney, was beatified. Arab priests came to sing in Syriac for his funeral. The timing felt like one of those through-a-glass-darkly moments, where something in the story is almost visible. But what you almost see doesn't take away the pain, doesn't fill the father's space, doesn't prove anything except that whatever story God is telling really does weigh down even the best human beings, or *especially* the best, with the heavy burden of a cross.

I said earlier that as I slowly improved I became conscious of my luck and blessings and good fortune—in the money that we had to lose, the family support, even the internet savvy that my career had trained me in. But the most basic blessing woven into the burden of a chronic illness has been the opportunity to keep going on, to remain there as a father and a husband even in a diminished state, to love my wife and watch my children and maybe someday their children rather than letting them go early, leaving them alone. Which was the thing I feared the most in those phantom heart attack moments, those emergency room trips: not my own death but my *absence,* not the end of my own story but my premature departure from theirs.

The chance to keep on going also includes the chance to keep fighting, to keep searching for answers, to keep hoping for a cure. Right now, for many sick people, that hope isn't answered—many people never have the breakthrough, never find a way to grind toward health, and simply slip into a permanent purgatory—and many chronic illnesses remain even more challenging to fight than Lyme. But my own experience makes me think that many more people *could* get better, many more people could be saved, in a system that encouraged sufferers to experiment at the margins of medical consensus—ideally more safely, with more supervision, than I did—rather than abandoning them to pain-relief medication and a mental-health diagnosis. At the very least we would have better doctors, a wiser medical apparatus, if there was greater recognition that the body is a permeable landscape in which many unknown enemies can lodge, and if more physicians were willing to approach medical treatment as a war in Sun Tzu's sense—not just a science but a difficult, interesting, experimental art.

I am writing this story in part for those chronically suffering, more numerous than the healthy ever realize—to give them hope that their condition can be changed even if it can't be eliminated, that they might be able to save their own lives even if they feel abandoned by their doctors, that they might, like me, be able to get, not fully well yet, but better, genuinely *better*.

But I am also writing for the skeptical doctors and doubtful experts who are so often the targets of long-suffering Lyme patients' fury and suspicion, in hopes of convincing them to see more clearly the enfleshed reality of a chronic, life-stealing disease.

In part of my mind, the evidence they are rejecting seems overwhelming. But in another part I can see—and have tried to explain—why they have remained so skeptical for so long.

I can stand outside my own situation, outside this testimony, and see how wild the whole story might sound—a bacterium that baffles blood tests, that shape-shifts and survives months of IV treatment, that produces such an absurd variety of symptoms, that requires treatments so complex and varied that they can't be easily studied in the double-blind controlled style, that leads patients to experiment with magnets and sound waves, with treatments that seem like witchcraft to the modern medical mind.

But I also know that the only reason I have slowly crawled my way up from hell is that all these strange things are connected to the strange reality of this disease, and all the strange experiments are the only way to save some patients from the pit.

It's completely understandable that the medical establishment doesn't want to officially endorse any of the various unproven paths. But there's a difference between declining to endorse a single path and ruling further treatment out entirely, a difference between acknowledging the diversity of case studies and claiming that no lessons can be drawn from the diverse attempts to treat them.

What chronic Lyme patients are asking of these skeptics is not a new certainty to replace the old one, not the endorsement of any single protocol or theory. What they are asking—what is entirely reasonable to ask in the face of so much suffering—is for doctors not to simply wash their hands of us, but to instead embrace the experimental spirit that chronic sickness seems to obviously require.

We aren't asking doctors to promise that they can definitively heal us. We are just asking them to try.

. . .

To strive, to seek, to find, and not to yield. That's from Tennyson, on the old age of heroes. I'm neither old nor heroic, but to get sick without a clear way to get better is to be asked to live up to a version of that admonition. The gift of chronic illness is the space and opportunity to strive and seek. The purpose of the illness in your life has to involve finding something—finding strength in learning how to endure, finding virtue in how to live for others, finding some hidden truth in unraveling the mystery of what actually ails you. And not to yield is often the hardest task of all.

I can't claim to have gained all the things I should have gained from the past six years. *Who will I be when this is over?* my mind would sometimes ask in the depths, since it was hard to imagine the same self that went into this illness coming out the other side. But now that I'm closer, God willing, to the end than the beginning, I can still recognize the person beneath the peeling dragon scales—maybe a little wiser, a little more patient, a little less consumed by the political, a little more open-minded, but still carrying many of the same habits and vices and temptations as the me I knew before.

But I have learned, at least, something about what it means *not to yield,* to go on searching and fighting and simply living in the shadow of despair, to do what must be done even when it seems like your body is incapable of the task and your mind is brutally imprisoned.

What doesn't kill you doesn't necessarily make you stronger. But what doesn't kill you *doesn't kill you,* and sometimes that alone supplies the thin reed of hope, the solid thing to cling to when every other help and possibility goes through your fingers like sand.

That first sickened summer in Maine, sixteen months into the illness, when nothing was working and my body blazed with pain, I forced myself to do what I would do as a child, to run along the packed brown surface of the sandbar, splashing through the inch of water rippling beneath my feet, and then suddenly pivot and stagger out deeper and fling myself up and out and down, belly-whopping into the freezing water of the bay.

For an instant or more, the shock to my system would be more pressing than the pain, and I would come up spluttering, every nerve jangling, and think: *I am still alive.*

I am still alive.

That's where this not-yet-finished story ends. I have lived for six years with invaders in my flesh, I have seen the world from way down underneath, I have done things I couldn't have imagined, I have fought and fought and fought.

And I am still alive.

ACKNOWLEDGMENTS

THIS BOOK AND, IN CERTAIN WAYS, ITS AUTHOR WOULD not exist without all of the uncountable human beings—doctors, researchers, and patients above all—who have dedicated themselves to fighting chronic Lyme disease, against an impenetrable-seeming wall of opposition and denial. I am grateful to each and every one of them, but especially to Steven Phillips for his wisdom and his patience; to Brian Fallon for advice and direction; and to Daniel Cameron, Carrie Hartney, and Jennifer Boyd for treatment. Also, among those I haven't met but learned from all the same: Pamela Weintraub, Marty Ross, Daniel Jaller, and various anonymous posters on flash.lymenet.org.

I am also grateful to everyone who helped my family survive our hardest time: Debbie Whitney, especially; Luis Fajardo, Jack Baldaserini, James Ahern, and the community at Apple Blossom. In the writing that followed, I'm indebted to Rafe Sagalyn, as always; to Derek Reed for seeing promise in the project; to Jackson Wolford for invaluable support.

Above all, I am grateful to my family and dear friends for a thousand different kinds of help and support: my father, my mother, my sister, Maureen, Julie, Judith and Steven, Alex, Brian, Allen, Praveen, Josh, Reihan, MBD, Rod, and Emily.

Also, if you're listening: Athanasius, Gregory, Wilbert Snow, Julie Douthat, the original Abigail, and Catherine Boyle.

I'm grateful to my children, Gwendolyn and Eleanor, Nicholas and Rosemary, for loving their father at his worst and hopefully only remembering the best.

And Abby, for everything, for always, I love you, let's never do anything like that again.

ABOUT THE AUTHOR

Ross Douthat has been an opinion columnist for *The New York Times* since 2009. Previously, he was a senior editor at *The Atlantic*. He is the author of *The Decadent Society, To Change the Church, Bad Religion,* and *Privilege;* the co-author, with Reihan Salam, of *Grand New Party;* and the film critic for *National Review*. He is a visiting fellow at the American Enterprise Institute, a media fellow at the Institute for Human Ecology at the Catholic University of America, and the writer-in-residence at the Elm Institute. He lives with his wife and four children in New Haven, Connecticut.

Twitter: @DouthatNYT